OUT OF COURT

How to Protect Your Business From Litigation

By John F. Landrum

The Headwaters Press, Inc.
New Orleans, Louisiana

The Headwaters Press, Inc.
331 Fairway Drive
New Orleans, Louisiana 70124

Printed in the United States of America

Library of Congress Pre-Assigned Catalogue No. 92-073418

ISBN 0-9633730-9-9

ACKNOWLEDGMENTS

In this book, the voice of experience is, in reality, a chorus. The author gratefully acknowledges the helpful suggestions of lawyers Ray Areaux, Stacy Brown, Steve Carleton, John Colbert, Grant Coleman, Frank Connolly, David Conroy, David Culpepper, Wanda Holloway, Jim Irvin, Harold Koretzky, Miriam Miller, Joe Schwertz, Charles Snyder, Frank Tessier and Talmage Watts. Except where expressly stated, the italicized anecdotes in this book are fictional. Any similarity to any existing person or actual incident is purely coincidental.

The book has also benefitted from the suggestions of Rob Bickham, Parke Ellis, Tripp Friedler, Leslie Jacobs, Scott Jacobs, Cathy Coleman Harris, Roger Kavanagh, William L. Kohlmann, Tony Ladt, Emily Landrum, Sam LeBlanc IV, Ann Mahorner, Kay Priestly and Leonard Wormser; from the editing of Nancy Eickel, Kevin McDermott and Jennifer Wieseneck; from the research of Sharon Robinson; from the publishing advices of Helen Dietrich, Patrick Gipson, William Griffin and Mindy Mayer; and from the design work of Karen Adjmi.

Finally, without the swift and accurate WordPerfect skills of Karen Schouest, Linda Jerkins and Ellen Ripp, the book would still be only a gleam in the author's eye.

NOTE

Women now make up approximately half of all law school classes. Earlier drafts of this book alternated the pronouns "he" and "she." The result was distracting. One cynical reader suggested that, for lawyers, the pronoun "it" would be a good compromise. Purely to avoid distracting the reader, the author has used masculine pronouns throughout the book.

TABLE OF CONTENTS

Table of Contents

Table of Contents

INTRODUCTION

Someone should hold a contest for the oldest lawyer joke. This one is surely a contender.

A famous heart surgeon died and ascended to Heaven. Waiting in line for admission, he grew impatient. A lawyer he had known on Earth walked past him in line. Saint Peter recognized the lawyer and made a great fuss over his arrival.

Exasperated, the heart surgeon left his place in line and approached Saint Peter. "Excuse me," he said. "I'm really not a complainer, but on Earth I saved lives every day. I've been standing in line for hours, and it's frustrating to see this lawyer walk right past me and be treated like a celebrity."

Saint Peter nodded sympathetically. "I know what you mean," he said. "But you have to understand, we don't get a lot of lawyers up here."

Lawyers certainly would be in trouble if getting into Heaven depended on popular election. The public outcry against lawyers and legal costs is louder than ever. On June 11, 1989, the *Washington Post* reported, "The past decade has seen legal costs at large firms skyrocket at nearly three times the rate of inflation, making legal representation almost beyond the ability of all but the wealthiest individuals and corporations to pay."

The *Post* continued:

> This excessively high cost has important repercussions throughout the entire economy. Considering that the combined gross revenue of the 30 firms profiled by the *National Law Journal* amounted to $3 billion, it is entirely reasonable to extrapolate that gross revenue for all large law firms could be five times that number.

Litigation in particular is to blame.

The loudest alarm bells are sounding for litigation costs. One writer in the October 19, 1990, issue of the *National Law Journal* estimates that American corporations spend $20 billion or more each year on litigation.

In an October 16, 1987, op-ed piece about the problem in the *New York Times*, United States Court of Appeals Judge Irving Kaufman criticized "the twin demons of expense and delay." Judge Kaufman quoted the legendary Judge Learned Hand, who stated over fifty years ago, "As a litigant, I should dread a lawsuit beyond almost anything else short of sickness and death." In Kaufman's view, the problem has only worsened. He noted: "For a small firm, skyrocketing litigation costs can sound its death knell."

Even those who profit from litigation -- lawyers themselves -- are beginning to see that its cost is too high. In the March 23, 1992, issue of the *Massachusetts Lawyers Weekly*, Stephen Paris, president of Defense Research

Institute, America's largest association of defense trial lawyers, referred to the "skyrocketing costs of litigation" and stated, "I would say that uppermost in the minds of defense lawyers today is probably the future of the civil jurisprudence system we have and the relationship between defense lawyers and their clients."

Our adversarial system makes litigation inefficient compared to transactional legal work.

You hear it so often: An ounce of prevention is worth a pound of cure. It is true for medicine. It is true for your car. It also happens to be true for law. In fact, litigation is even worse than other forms of cure. Because of the adversarial nature of litigation, the differences between preventive costs and curative costs in law are even greater than in other contexts. Imagine an operating room where the surgeon removing your gall bladder must contend against another surgeon who is dedicated to stopping him!

Money invested in legal advice during the transactional stage goes further than it does during litigation.

In negotiating a deal (putting aside hostile mergers and acquisitions, which can be more like litigation than other transactional negotiations), the parties usually have strong reasons to work together. Litigation, by contrast, is warfare. Unless you are a plaintiff worried about the other side's ability to pay, one of your very aims is to wear the other side down. You try to exhaust his war-chest and his willingness to fight.

In litigation, little is easy, and nothing is cheap. Both sides act and communicate guardedly and inefficiently. Documents that the other side once shared freely can now be obtained only by a formal pleading, often contested at great cost. Also, because you are in a war and because the rules of this war are so intricate, many of your activities are scheduled to suit someone else: the court, the jury, the witnesses, the other lawyers.

In litigation, the lawyer and client lose much of their power to bargain with each other.

Outside of litigation -- to get a document prepared or to seek advice on a deal -- you can usually bargain with your business lawyer to determine roughly what you will get and what you will pay for it. However, in litigation, much of what your lawyer must do is controlled not by you, but by the other side. Because so much of litigation work is done in response to the moves of the other side, it is hard to make informed decisions in advance about what the costs will be, and bargain with your lawyer accordingly.

Litigation forces you to pay experts to do non-expert work.

A lawyer's value lies in his knowledge. You wouldn't dream of paying a lawyer $150 per hour to mop your floors. He earns his hourly fee *only* when he has spent an hour using his knowledge for your benefit. However, in litigation, many activities require your lawyer's presence for their entire duration, but only use his wisdom for small parts of that time. For example, at a day-long deposition in a multi-party case, as much as half of the deposition time may be given to questions posed by other lawyers -- not yours -- with little impact on your position. During this time, you are paying your litigator $150 per hour to look out the window. It's not the litigator's fault. He can't arrange to be in the deposition only when his expertise is actually needed. Compared to transaction lawyers, the lengths of time in which a litigator "stands and waits" are far greater.

A business which spends money on litigation is wasting its resources.

For these and other reasons, litigation has an inflationary effect on your legal dollar. For example, the same commercial loan which the lender pays the lawyer $5000 to document may cost $100,000 to collect in court proceedings. Litigation turns your dollars into nickels.

Running a business requires you to know something about a lot of things. How to protect your business from litigation should be at the top of your list.

How to use this book.

This book is not another "do-it-yourself" kit, or another summary of business law. It is not an "exposé" of lawyers or law practice. Instead, the book explains how the economics of litigation and of the legal industry affect you. It explores how you can manage your business to reduce or even avoid the negative impact of these realities.

Introduction

Section One of this book explores cost-effective ways to prevent disputes:

o the role of ethics and of legal compliance;

o how insensitivity can increase your exposure;

o the importance of screening your business relationships; and

o how to structure deals to avoid litigation.

Section Two explains the role of "business lawyers" in helping you stay out of litigation:

o what business lawyers do and how to find the right one;

o the economics of using business lawyers; and

o how to work with them for best results.

Section Three explores ways to solve problems without litigating:

o the economics and mechanics of settlement negotiation;

o how such devices as arbitration and mediation can prevent disputes from becoming unnecessarily expensive; and

○ when to consider asking government authorities to litigate for you.

Section Four tells you what to do when you have to litigate:

○ how to find a litigator;

○ how to structure your litigator's compensation;

○ how to benefit from case plans and budgets;

○ how to use bills to monitor a case and expenses;

○ how to manage litigation to keep costs under control; and

○ how to learn from litigation.

Section One

THE FOUR PRINCIPLES OF LITIGATION AVOIDANCE

Litigation is war. Just as shooting wars can destroy a country, litigation can bankrupt your business. How do you stay out of it?

A schoolchild knows that the surest way to avoid getting a black eye is to stay out of fights. This wisdom does not follow everyone into adulthood. The effort which businesses give to avoiding litigation is often piecemeal and after-the-fact.

To avoid litigation, think of four concepts. The first is to act ethically, to comply with the law and to honor your contracts ("Do the Right Thing"). The second is to avoid creating the emotional atmosphere that leads to litigation ("Don't Be a Jerk"). The third is to recognize and avoid dealing with the sorts of people most likely to drag you into litigation ("Don't Hang Around with Jerks"). The fourth is to structure your relationships to reduce the opportunities for disputes and the incentives to litigate ("Do the Thing Right").

1

Always ask:

1. How can you be more sure that you comply with the law and meet your obligations?

2. How can you avoid raising someone's emotional interest in suing you?

3. How can you make sure that you are dealing with someone who has the integrity, ability and intelligence to reduce the chances that you will someday have to litigate?

4. How can you structure the deal or organize your enterprise to reduce the opportunities or incentives to litigate?

These principles are not about absolutes. Each applies to different businesses differently. The four principles are most useful -- and less intimidating -- if you think of them as a way of raising your consciousness. Use them to set priorities. If you forget the details of Section One, remember the chapter titles. They are good concepts for your business to live by.

Staying out of court does not require you to sacrifice principles, or to let yourself be pushed around. Usually, the opposite is true. One of the surest rules in avoiding litigation is to put yourself as often as you can in a position of strength.

Aside from helping to keep you out of court, these principles will also increase your chances of winning, and lower your costs when you do litigate.

Chapter One

Do the Right Thing

You are sitting in your lawyer's office. In ten minutes, your deposition is scheduled to begin. You and your lawyer are going over your testimony one more time. She is peering over the top of her glasses at you. After a long silence, she speaks. "That's not what you said the last time we talked about this and it's not what we said in our pleadings."

"Look," you respond. "I'm telling the truth as I remember it. If you don't believe me, you shouldn't represent me."

"I do believe you," she answers coolly. "That has nothing to do with it. What matters is that you have to be consistent. This is a swearing contest. If the other side has you on record as saying two different things, they'll tear you apart."

You look out the window. You would rather be anywhere else in the universe. When you leased your warehouse building to Suitprone eight years ago, you really cannot remember what you said about your property's environmental condition. You had no idea it had any significance. If the law made it so important, why did no one ever tell you?

Unless you ask, no one will. To understand the parts of the law that most affect your business, you have to take a proactive role. You can greatly lessen your chances of being sued by *doing the right thing*.

This may not be what you hoped to read. Perhaps you hoped to learn magic potions and secret passwords. If so, you may find some later parts of the book more gratifying. But do not fast forward yet.

Businesses often bring litigation on themselves.

You have probably read about frivolous litigation -- suits filed without any basis. Certainly frivolous litigation is a threat. But consider this: a large percentage of lawsuits against businesses are won by the *plaintiff* -- the person suing. In each of these cases, a judge or jury has concluded that the *defendant* -- the person being sued -- has done something wrong.

Most lawsuits (ninety percent) never get to trial, but *settle*. In a settlement, the defendant pays the plaintiff some part of the claim, and the plaintiff gives up his right to sue. A few settlements are for the *cost of defense*. In this kind of settlement, the defendant merely pays the plaintiff an estimate of the cost of defending the suit. A cost of defense settlement generally means that the suit has little merit. However, cost of defense settlements make up only a small part of all settlements. This means that most settling defendants see a reasonable chance that a judge or jury would find that they have done something wrong.

In other words, frivolous suits are not the only thing causing businesses to litigate.

4

The two components of doing the right thing.

Doing the right thing has two parts:

1. Ethical behavior.

2. Legal compliance.

1. Ethical Behavior and "Win-Win" Transactions.

One way to tell whether you are doing the right thing is the *smell test*.

○ Are you getting something for nothing?

○ Are you profiting from your business relationship because you are delivering something of value? Or merely because you have hidden something from the other side?

○ How would you like to be the person you are dealing with?

The biblical "golden rule" is a good way to predict whether a judge or jury will be on your side. If all the facts were made known (in litigation, they usually are), would you be embarrassed?

Doing the right thing goes far beyond simply not telling lies. The secret is to create win-win situations. Make the other side glad to have its relationship with you.

As you squeeze that last drop of profit out of a relationship, you may be crossing the line where the chances of litigation outweigh the gain. In fact, if others do not consistently benefit from their relationships with you, then you probably have an unhealthy enterprise in the first place. Litigation will only be one of the symptoms.

2. <u>Legal Compliance</u>.

What a world we might have if ethical behavior and delivering value were *all* it took to stay out of court! Unfortunately, another major problem is the complexity of the law that applies to many businesses. Improving your legal compliance requires three steps:

o   de-mystify the law;

o   take advantage of experts; and

o   make sure your knowledge is put into action.

a. <u>De-mystify the Law</u>.

Overcome the notion that the law is only for specialists. The law is the set of rules by which society plays. Imagine growing up in a house where your brothers and sisters knew the rules, but you did not!

Use publications.

Subscribe to trade journals, business magazines, or other publications that discuss legal developments in your field. No matter what your industry is, there is almost certainly a useful reference source available to you.

A number of law firms produce newsletters for their clients -- many in specific areas such as labor law, construction law, tax law or intellectual property. An attorney friend will usually be glad to send you any newsletters that his firm generates.

Attend seminars.

Many seminars for lawyers are also suitable for non-lawyers. If you already have an attorney, or simply know one, ask him to send you any brochures he receives for seminars which may have some bearing on you or your business.

Understand the obligations you have accepted.

You are also bound by the contracts you have signed. Do you understand your loan agreement? Your lease? Your partnership agreement?

Consider formal education.

Would it be out of the question for you to attend a business law course of a college or business school? The American Management Association holds classes in many cities for managers in every industry. Other organizations offer courses on such topics as hiring and employee relationships. Many of these teaching groups share mailing lists.

Tailor your compliance efforts to your circumstances.

You need not master every part of the law that may apply to your enterprise. Decide how much education it is cost-effective for you to obtain. Look for cheaper methods of reaching the same result. For example, if your time is really at a premium, consider asking a partner, an associate or one of your employees to learn more about the law and help your business comply.

b. Take Advantage of Experts.

Use accountants to help identify issues.

Good accountants do not offer legal advice. However, a good accountant can help tremendously in spotting issues that justify more concentrated compliance efforts. This can be a fringe benefit of using a CPA regularly.

Use engineers and architects to avoid personal injury, property damage, and public accommodation liability.

If you manufacture a product that can injure people or property, or if you operate a physical plant for manufacturing or retailing, consult engineers or architects familiar with safety standards and workplace regulations such as those issued by OSHA. More and more architects are also becoming familiar with the Americans with Disabilities Act, which sets mandatory standards for making places of public accommodation accessible to the disabled.

Take advantage of an insurer's loss-control program.

Insurers are becoming more aggressive in helping their insureds to control liabilities. Loss-control programs are most active in preventing property damage and bodily injury. If you own or operate a building where employees work or customers shop, your insurer may send an engineer to look for hazards and ways to mitigate them. If you sell a product, your insurer may prescribe warning labels or even safer designs to prevent product-liability claims. If you operate vehicles, the insurer may recommend driver and fleet maintenance programs.

Loss control is also gaining importance in preventing other types of liabilities. The insurer who issues a business liability policy may ask to see your most important contracts to look for problems such as one-sided indemnity clauses. If you have a large advertising budget, the insurer may review your ads for "red flags" indicating possible defamation or unfair trade practices.

Talk to a property/casualty insurance agent, whether an independent or a direct writer for a single insurer. If the premiums and coverages justify it, most insurers will do a loss-control program free of charge (if not, it can often be worth buying). In the process, insurers not only protect themselves; they may also warn you of liabilities excluded from coverage. If your premium or coverage is so small that the insurer will not give priority to your loss-control program, many insurance agents will help you look for problems.

Take advantage of regulatory outreach programs.

Most federal agencies have public information services available in Washington, D.C. Several have offices in major cities. Funding scarcities make many of them as anxious as you are to avoid litigation. For this reason, many agencies will help you in your efforts to comply. For example, the Equal Employment Opportunity Commission and many others will take telephone calls and discuss issues on an anonymous basis.

Consult business lawyers early.

Informal advice from a regulator is not binding and does not preclude regulatory action. For any issue -- regulatory or not -- with high stakes or great complexity, use a lawyer. Section Two of this book describes how to find and hire a business lawyer. It also suggests ways to keep the cost of business lawyers under control, so that you are not deterred from investing in the long-term savings which they can make possible.

c. Put Your Knowledge into Action.

Often, your employees or partners will need to benefit from your litigation-avoidance knowledge. Some companies ask their lawyer(s) to give occasional lunch presentations. Others find that one of their own employees, if properly briefed, communicates with his colleagues more effectively. Whoever leads these "seances," ask him to prioritize the issues and to avoid jargon. Use up-to-date teaching methods such as videotape.

On the other side, do whatever you can to make the audience receptive. Make sure everyone understands that your business's survival may depend on staying out of court. Consider giving rewards for avoiding litigation.

Don't just go through the motions.

Employee relationships are the greatest source of litigation for many businesses. Wage/hour disputes, EEOC claims and OSHA violations all share much of the credit.

If your company has more than a few employees, you should probably know what regulators mean by these terms:

AAP	Color	At will employee
ADA	Creed	Disciplinary action
ADEA	Merit	Employment contract
EEOC	Race	Open-door policy
OSHA	Sex	Whistle-blower

For regulated employers and even for smaller shops, well-considered and written policies are one of the best forms of prevention. However, this is only true if they are meaningful and result in actual compliance. Don't just "walk the walk and talk the talk."

Shout it from the roof tops.

Once you have done what it takes to obey the law, publicize your efforts. For example, get your employment policy into every employee's hands. Again, use teaching tools such as videotape to emphasize high points. This educates your potential adversary so that he brings fewer frivolous claims. You are also better off if he knows how to resolve arguably valid complaints. After you work with an employee to resolve a complaint, get his input for possible changes of policy.

If you try, it's easier than you think.

Too many people think that understanding the law is beyond reach. The most important hurdles are simply knowing how to get access to information which is readily available and making the commitment to do so. A good number of business people *do* have a working knowledge of the rules that govern their business. For those who do understand the law and try to follow it, their legal cost relative to their revenues is generally less.

Chapter Two

Don't Be a Jerk

You find a message on your voice mailbox from a buyer of your telephone system. He states that his system was down for a full day. He claims that the breakdown cost him a $20,000 sale.

You remember working with your lawyer to include in the standard sale agreement a disclaimer that excluded your liability for "consequential damages," including economic losses due to breakdowns. Feeling comfortable that you have no liability, you feel free to ignore your customer's calls. The calls are soon followed by a demand letter, which you also regard as frivolous and ignore.

Soon after, you are served with a summons and complaint. When you call your lawyer, he agrees that you should have no liability. He prepares an answer and moves to dismiss the lawsuit on the basis of the disclaimer. However, your opponent is quite angry. He wins the court's permission to take discovery on the negotiations leading up to the sale agreement, and discovery on your treatment of similar claims in the past. During the discovery process, no particularly damaging facts emerge, and your lawyer eventually prevails on the motion to dismiss.

13

So why shouldn't you be happy? The answer is that you have spent legal fees of $5000 to $15,000. A different approach would have likely saved most or all of this cost.

Dear John:

I have received your message, in which you indicated that a breakdown in your telephone system caused you to lose a sale. You will recall that our sale agreement specifically excluded consequential damages resulting from breakdowns, including lost customers. This was necessary because of the difficulty at our end in predicting and controlling any loss of customers that might result from a failure in the equipment we sell. Our pricing was based in part on this exclusion.

Nevertheless, I am always distressed when a customer complains of a failure in one of our systems. I hope you will allow one of our specialists to inspect your system, free of charge, to determine whether the cause was a power failure in your building (the most common problem) or a defect in the system or in the installation itself. Rest assured that we will make every effort to determine the source and advise how to prevent its recurrence.

Sincerely,
John Doe
John Doe Telephone Systems, Inc.

This chapter discusses how ignoring personality issues (being a "jerk") can land you in court.

You will not be a "jerk" if you follow these rules:

1. Communicate your concern for others;

2. Don't put people in impossible positions; and

3. Don't be a part of the litigation problem.

1. Communicate your Concern for Others.

Litigation is like murder -- it requires not only opportunity, but motive as well.

Even the most dangerous poisonous snake is as afraid of you as you are of it. The snake is likely to bite only when it is cornered or surprised. Similarly, many people with valid claims against you may think of litigation with the same fear and loathing that you do.

People sue you because they feel you have wronged them. Even a person with a very weak claim may ignore his lawyer's advice and sue you if you have offended him personally. You can often avoid litigation with a prompt response, an expression of sympathy, and a sincere effort to help.

A few years ago, a Japanese airliner crashed. Within hours, the president of the airline had spoken with the families of every victim. The company president also resigned to atone for the disaster, which he accepted as his personal responsibility. Every victim's family settled without a lawsuit.

Cynics may respond that this could never happen here; that our litigation system would not let it. On the other hand, if gestures like these were more common, maybe our litigation system would not be what it is.

Accepting responsibility can improve your business reputation.

The evidence suggests that communicating a sense of personal responsibility will be rewarded, even in America. In *The Dynamics of Bargaining Games* (Prentice Hall 1991), J. Keith Murnighan tells the story of a construction company that was building a new football stadium. When a beam collapsed during construction, the company president held a news conference to state that his company was fully to blame. After the press conference, the construction company was flooded with new business. Apparently, the new customers were impressed by the show of honesty.

A colleague joined a law firm that had slowly been losing its share of a particular client's work. Shortly after arriving at the firm, he had to handle a matter for that client when the client's usual contacts at the firm were out of town. The associate had been warned that this client was "difficult." The client called to see if an information package had arrived. The associate replied that it had not, but offered to check with the mailroom just in case. On checking, the associate learned that the package had been misrouted after arriving at the firm. The associate called to report finding the package. The client asked, "Who messed up? Us or you?" The associate answered, "I think at our end the left hand just didn't know what the right hand was doing." The client said, "I can't tell you how refreshing it is to get a little honesty." The firm began to win back the client's business, with the associate as the lead contact.

Overcome the instinctive fear of accepting responsibility.

Perhaps it is instinctive to deny wrongdoing. One mistake, you think, may be all it takes to lose future business. To prevent that, you fight any complaints to the bitter end.

Put yourself in the other side's shoes. Most people know that even the best businesses make mistakes. However, when you *are* clearly wrong, and still deny fault, they can only draw two conclusions:

1. You believe what you are saying (message: you are unreasonable or incompetent); or

2. You do *not* believe what you are saying (message: you are dishonest).

In either case, you lose credibility. The real test is not to show you never make mistakes. Instead, people judge you by how you respond to the errors that you -- like everyone else -- make.

Understand the importance of relationships.

A seller of advertising space for a radio station once put it this way: "Behind every complaint is a commitment." When someone complains to you, he is expressing an investment in what you do. By complaining, he has added to that investment. This is not a person to shrug off! He is giving you an opportunity.

Responding to complaints in a positive way does more than control the damage; it can *strengthen* your relationship. Thomas Peters and Robert H. Waterman, Jr., in their best-selling book *In Search of Excellence* (Warner Books 1988), found that companies with perennially strong performances tended to be those that were most responsive to their customers.

Do you treat relationships like disposable diapers? When one becomes soiled, do you simply turn your attention to the next? In Japan, litigation is treated as an extreme last resort because it destroys relationships. Japanese businesses regard relationships as one of their most valuable assets. *A solid relationship is also the best insurance you will ever have against litigation.*

You act through your employees.

Watch how your employees affect your company's relationships. If you see a problem, consider rotating in another person as the lead contact. Once again, litigation avoidance goes hand-in-glove with good business. According to Peters and Waterman, another hallmark of successful companies is that the employees love the customers.

Understand how your actions affect relationships.

Sometimes you may offend others without ever knowing it. If you are entering a new kind of relationship, understand the customs that people bring to that relationship. If you are overseeing an employee for the first time, you may be unfamiliar with certain employee benefits that are not legally required, but which are often expected. For example, laying someone off without severance pay may change his attitude toward you.

If you are new to a business, understand the trade usages and customs in your industry. *Don't be a jerk through lack of sophistication.*

Communicating your concern to others helps you win when you do go to court.

Following this advice does more than ward off suits. When you *are* sued, personality issues play a role in deciding who wins. This is especially true in jury trials. For example, evidence that you are rude to employees will increase the chances of a jury ruling against you in a close employment-law case.

2. __Don't Put People in Impossible Positions.__

Beware of putting someone in a position where he has no choice but to go for your jugular.

You may think it is to your advantage to frighten the daylights out of your opponent. It is usually wiser to leave him with something. Even when you are right, beware of creating situations where someone's only choices are his own destruction or yours. As the saying goes, there are few things more dangerous than a cornered dog.

3. __Don't be a Part of the Litigation Problem.__

Not being a "jerk" goes beyond warding off litigation by others. It has another side. Do *you* needlessly involve people in litigation?

- o Do you constantly disagree with others about the meaning of your contracts?

- o Do people have to sue you to collect valid debts?

- o Do you sue others, hoping to force a quick settlement?

- o Do you react emotionally when the unexpected occurs?

20

○   Do you see yourself as a rugged individu-
    alist, when others consider you a real
    problem?

If you are any of these people, don't blame lawyers
alone for the booming litigation industry. If you are not
one of these people, the following chapter will help you
steer clear of those who are.

Chapter Three

Don't Hang Around with Jerks

You are putting together a venture capital group. Each of the limited partners will put up cash, together with a note for additional sums. One of the participants, Mr. Megabucks, is a multi-millionaire rancher-oilman in Texas. Although Megabucks' financial statements are impressive, you know that he is attempting to renegotiate a large existing loan with Bigbank, his lender, due to another recent drop in oil prices and slowed royalties. Megabucks reassures you, "Don't worry about Bigbank. I've instructed my lawyer to threaten them with a multi-million dollar lender liability claim. They will not be a problem."

You chuckle. What a guy to have in your foxhole! The deal is done.

One year later, Megabucks is five months overdue on his notes to the partnership. Efforts to negotiate a workout have failed. Your partnership has told Megabucks that it plans to sue.

Your secretary calls you to the reception area, where you are handed a complaint filed by Megabucks against the partnership and against you personally. The complaint claims that you violated the security laws. Megabucks' complaint also seeks to have his promissory notes to the partnership declared invalid, and also demands millions in damages. You are in for the fight of your life.

In hindsight, it seems so obvious. But Megabucks and you got along so well. It was hard to imagine him dealing with you the same way he dealt with Bigbank.

Smart businesses don't hang around with jerks. Watch out for four different kinds:

1.   The bad hiring choice;

2.   The financially troubled;

3.   The dishonest or irresponsible; and

4.   The inexperienced or irrational.

1. <u>The Bad Hiring Choice</u>

With the possible exception of fellow owners, no relationship will be more important than those you have with your employees. Employees are more likely to sue you than anyone else. They also can be the source of many of your liabilities to third parties. If employees play a significant role in your operations, there is no substitute for getting the advice of a lawyer specializing in employment and labor law. He can offer screening advice. He can also tell you which screening devices are illegal. Not as a substitute for seeing a lawyer, but to get you started, here are a few thoughts.

1. Get the applicant's written consent to seek information from personal references, former employers, and other sources.

2. Get a written waiver and release from liability in connection with reference checks.

3. Inspect all information provided by an applicant, looking carefully for suspicious or unusual entries or omissions.

4. Look for gaps in employment history. Check job titles and dates of tenure carefully.

5. Get a written release from the applicant to verify education degrees.

6. Contact each previous employer and personal reference listed on the application.

7. Ask all former employers and personal references if they have any reason to doubt that the applicant is reliable, honest and trustworthy, and check to see if they are aware if the applicant has been engaged in a violent act, has a violent temper, or has a past criminal conviction.

8. Ask each former employer and personal reference to name one or two more references. This way, you can make sure that the one you are checking is not recommending the applicant out of bias or intimidation.

9. Document all information received from previous employers and personal references.

10. Document all *efforts* to obtain information from previous employers and personal references, especially if information was not obtainable from such sources.

11. Consider whether the nature of the employment justifies a criminal record search.

12. Perform reference checks even on temporary or casual employees.

13. Re-evaluate an employee's fitness for a position if the employee is changing jobs within your organization.

There are a number of private companies that will do screening for you, either independently or in coordination with your own procedures. Some insurers will recommend drug screening services or offer advice on hiring practices.

Multiple interviews give you a look over time at your prospective employee. It is probably a good idea to do at least three.

Peters and Waterman report that "excellent" companies do intense screening. According to Peters and Waterman, some bring recruits back for seven or eight interviews.

Screening employees carefully just makes good sense. Both in preventing litigation and in making your business work, employees *are* your company.

2. The Financially Troubled Counterparty.

When insolvencies require assets to be divided, you will pay lawyers to protect your rights against the debtor or against third-party creditors. In measuring the risk against your expected return, think about more than the amount at stake and the chances of loss. Consider the attorneys fees that might be spent to protect your interests as well.

Do your underwriting homework.

Reputation is very meaningful. Ask around. Check with the credit bureau, or Dun & Bradstreet. If possible, ask for financial statements, with both balance sheets and income and expense reports. Financial statements are much more reliable if audited. If the financial statements are not audited, ask for recent federal income tax returns, too. Make sure that the only discrepancies are due to differences between the accounting methods that apply to tax returns, on the one hand, and those that apply to financial statements, on the other. If income tax returns are unavailable, ask for quarterly payroll or sales tax reports. Your accountant or banker can help you interpret whatever

26

you receive. Your banker can also refer you to commercial firms that do asset searches for private parties.

3. The Dishonest or Irresponsible Counterparty.

Some businesses use litigation as a way of renegotiating their contracts. A building developer may accept a bid that he knows is over his budget. The developer brings the cost back to budget at the end of construction by claiming damages for delay or for defects. The contractor is in a poor bargaining position; he needs to be paid and settle with his subcontractors. He accepts a "haircut" as better than litigating.

A contracting company that is closing its operations in a region may shortchange its remaining projects in that area. The company hopes that the cost of litigating will deter claims for defective workmanship or excessive delay.

Jerks act on the theory that their deceptions will go unprosecuted or even unnoticed. Jerks take unwarranted stands in litigation which needlessly add to its expense. Some use litigation to prioritize their debts. Only a creditor with the will and ability to pursue them will get paid.

Look for integrity.

Your business attorney may form some judgments about your counterparty. After a negotiating session, ask for his impressions.

27

Again, reputation can be a valuable tool. Evidence of dishonesty in the negotiation phase is also a clear warning. Take seriously any references to underhanded dealings with others. Anyone who jokes with you about pulling a fast one on somebody else is a problem waiting to happen. It is almost always a mistake to think that the power of your personality will protect you.

Watch out for those who "protest too much."

A veteran litigator of fraud cases says that whenever he is asking questions at a deposition, and the other side begins his answer with "Honestly" or "To tell the truth," he becomes suspicious. This intuition has a basis in logic. Why would someone who is consistently truthful need to tell you he is not lying? Look hard at people who talk too much about their own honesty.

4. <u>The Inexperienced or Irrational.</u>

A final kind of jerk is the inexperienced or the irrational. Once a dispute begins, he acts unreasonably and makes a fair settlement impossible.

Look for evidence of reasonableness.

Again, look at reputation. What do past business associates say? Also screen for this type of jerk with thorough discussions of the deal. Discuss the benefits expected by either side and the events that could upset the deal. This kind of discussion may show how the other side will react later if problems surface.

Computerized Screening Devices.

Most law firms have access to computerized data systems, such as LEXIS or WESTLAW. Many accounting firms have LEXIS and a few have WESTLAW. Either system can be searched for references to your counterparty in any major periodical and in most trade journals. You can even authorize a case name search in LEXIS or WESTLAW to give you a good idea of how many times this party has been in litigation. For publicly traded companies, you can get quarterly and annual reports summarizing financial information and describing material litigation. For privately held companies, other less extensive data is often available. WESTLAW offers Dunn & Bradstreet reports. All of this is cheaper and easier than you may think.

A newer system gaining popularity with law firms and banks is the NDX on-line court access system. This service allows you to search directly into court records to see if someone has been involved in any suit as recently as twenty-four hours earlier. You can even look for any property lien or levy that has been filed into the court records.

The Economics of Screening your Counterparty.

It is not suggested that you never do business with anyone who could possibly pull you into a lawsuit. If you have constant small transactions with many customers, you may be better off just making some allowance for bad debts, rather than doing intense screening.

Think of a sliding scale, with small-volume customers or vendors at one end, and close, long-term relationships, such as those with partners or employees, at the other. As you move up the scale, your screening should increase. Unless your relationship is minor, screening is the proverbial ounce of prevention. Litigation is the pound of cure.

There is a joke about a small town with one litigator. In the joke, the litigator was starving until a second lawyer moved to town. Then they both became rich.

The unfortunate truth is, one litigator can do fairly well. All he needs is a client of the kind described in this chapter.

Chapter Four

Do the Thing Right

A contracting company agrees with the county to re-excavate a canal. The specifications in the county's invitation to bid are based on soil samples from the surface of the dry land next to the canal. The contractor expects that the actual conditions in the canal bottoms will be different from the samples. The contractor also assumes that, once the amount of the muck in the canal bottom becomes measurable, the county will negotiate in good faith to raise the contract price. Instead, the county refuses to recognize differing site conditions. The contractor abandons the project to force a compromise. By the time the county authorizes the extra work, the delay has substantially increased the contractor's overhead for the job. At the same time, two attorneys have profited handsomely.

Both sides would have paid the lawyers less, and used them more effectively, if the contractor had insisted on samples from the canal bottom, and based the contract price on those samples. Better yet, the contractor and county could have agreed from the start to a per-unit price for the quantity of muck that the actual conditions required the contractor to dig. They could also have named an objective way to measure the requirements. The contractor *finessed* the issue because he feared he would not get the job. Instead, he got a job which brought a net loss.

Don't shy away from confronting issues in transacting.

There is often a tension between the desire to close a deal, and the need to do the deal right. The thinking is something like, "If problems arise, the other side will be reasonable," or "I don't want to insult them."

This kind of reasoning has a logical flaw. If planning for problems insults your counterparty, that is a signal that this person *will not be reasonable* if problems should arise. If trying to negotiate a clear deal turns the other side off, this is probably the sort of person you should avoid.

Even if the other side shares your desire to think the contract through, the discussion itself may unearth issues that you cannot resolve. It is better to find these before putting your signature on a contract.

The three concepts of Doing the Thing Right.

In shaping your transactions, remember three concepts:

1. Preempt disagreements through communication and planning.

2. Create disincentives to litigate.

3. Draft the contract to make litigation less expensive.

1. Preempt Disagreements Through Communication and Planning.

Make sure your agreement is clear.

Do you have a clear idea of what your product can and cannot do? Does the buyer have a clear idea? Is the buyer's idea the same as yours? Or does your warranty contain a long fine-print set of exclusions which the buyer has not read?

Do you have a clear idea of what is required under your agreement? Does the other side have a clear idea? Are your ideas the same? What could go wrong and prevent one side from living up to his side of the bargain? Do you agree on what the consequences would be? Does the contract reflect your agreement? Can you show your agreement to a neutral third party and get him to draw the same interpretation as you do?

The question is: Do you and your counterparty have a meeting of the minds?

Document your negotiations and save correspondence.

If oral understandings form an important part of the negotiations, confirm them clearly in writing. Otherwise, years later when a dispute arises, one of you may not remember them. Is there a good reason not to make these understandings a part of the agreement? (If there *is* a good reason, put the reason in writing too.)

Save all correspondence written before and after signing an agreement. The rules of evidence limit the admissibility of such documents in court. However, these rules, referred to collectively as the *parol evidence rule,* have so many exceptions that the documents often are allowed as evidence. In arbitration, furthermore, the strict rules of evidence do not usually apply.

Often, this correspondence will be enough to remind a good-faith counterparty of your original intent, making litigation or arbitration unnecessary.

Be careful of subjectivity in your transaction.

Many kinds of contracts require one or both sides to act *reasonably.* Even where the contract does not, the law may impose a duty to act in *good faith.* In some cases these requirements are necessary and good. However, subjective requirements can also breed disputes. Try to identify the dangers that make *reasonableness* necessary. Is there a way to rework the relationship to get rid of the danger?

If a reasonableness standard *is* necessary, maybe you can at least come up with some clear basis for deciding what *is* reasonable. If not, can you give a neutral referee the power to decide questions of reasonableness?

In an agreement to license technology, for example, the licensor may want some assurance that the licensee will get the product to market before it becomes "stale." For that reason, some agreements provide that the licensee will develop the product with *reasonable* diligence. Consider using a minimum royalty payment instead, so that the licensee is losing money while he delays development. Another option is to set time frames for specific steps in development, such as regulatory approval. A third alternative is to designate, in advance, a neutral expert to determine whether the licensee's diligence is reasonable.

In a different example, employee terminations are often challenged for cause. In some states, an employment contract with no stated term, or with no list of grounds for firing, is *terminable at will* -- that is, without cause. In other states, the contract must affirmatively state that it is terminable at will. If your employment contract is not made terminable at will, either by law or by agreement, then you may face a disagreeable choice: either to let a bad employee stay or risk a suit for wrongful discharge. Try to solve the problem in advance with the right kind of employment agreement.

"Walk through" any contractual formula.

Many agreements use some kind of formula for pricing or for payments. Other contracts -- particularly loan agreements -- establish minimum earnings and net worth floors, or ceilings on indebtedness. Whenever your agreement uses a formula, walk through two or three hypotheticals with your counterparty. Make sure that the formula actually works and that you both apply it the same way. While it is not usually feasible to include the examples in the agreement, save the written examples in case questions later arise.

Allocate risks to the party best able to prevent them.

To discourage the kind of problems that create disputes, allocate the risk of such problems to the party who is best able to prevent them.

For example, in a technology licensing agreement, the licensee is sometimes in the better position to prevent product liability claims. When that is true, try to make the licensee responsible for product-liability insurance. Then, to the extent that product-liability claims arise, the licensee will bear the increased premium expense.

Similarly, in a royalty agreement or distributorship agreement, the licensee or distributor is often in the better position to shape the market for the product. When that is true, shift as much of the market risk as you can to the licensee or distributor. It is seldom possible--and often undesirable--to shift all market risk. But increased license or franchise fees, balanced against lower royalty rates, can help put the incentives where the ability lies.

2. <u>Create Reasons Not to Litigate</u>.

Make your relationship more valuable to the other side than the benefits of litigation.

After your contract is executed and performance begins, the value of creating "win-win" situations only grows. If you are guilty of a technical default, you may escape any penalty if it is not in the other side's interest to make it an issue.

If your counterparty is "winning" (or believes he will eventually "win") because of his relationship with you, then he has every reason to work out conflicts that arise. On the other hand, if he realizes he has made a bad deal, he may look for the first chance to make an issue out of a performance problem.

Consider attorneys fee clauses.

In England, the loser pays the other side's attorneys fees as a matter of course. Most experts agree that the *English Rule* reduces lawsuits. In America, attorneys fees are recoverable only in a few kinds of cases. However, you can often agree in your contract to use the English Rule. Your contract can provide that if either side has to litigate to enforce its rights, the winner will recover its attorneys fees.

Chapter Three discussed the danger of associating with litigious counterparties. A clause requiring the losing party in litigation to pay the other's attorneys fees provides some insurance against your failure to screen for that trait. Of course, the clause will only help you if you are less likely than the other side to take an unwarranted position. That is, you are betting that you will be less of a *jerk* than he is.

Consider an arbitration clause.

Arbitration is usually faster and cheaper than ordinary litigation. Chapter Seven explains arbitration fully. Will disputes under this contract involve mainly technical matters which can be decided in good faith without total war? If so, consider including an arbitration clause.

Shift the burden of litigating to others.

Is there some way to make whatever problem arises someone else's problem? Will insurance, a bond, a guarantee, or a letter of credit, save you from having to litigate?

Insurance companies routinely defend claims. Without the same organization and staff, defending a claim may be more troublesome and expensive for you. Also, as insurers pay more attention to loss control, involving a liability insurer can benefit both of you. There is no substitute for consulting a reputable agent who understands your industry to decide what liabilities you should insure.

One danger in collection suits may be that the other side has concealed assets. Locating and seizing such assets can be expensive and take time. Collection is easier if a third party with financial strength will guarantee the other side's obligations. If the guarantee is properly drafted, you can sue the guarantor directly without first exhausting your buyer's assets. The guarantor can then decide whether he wants to seek reimbursement at his own expense. Performance bonds and letters of credit can often be used in a similar way.

3.   Draft the Contract to Make Litigation Less Expensive.

There are number of other things you can do in the transactional stage to lessen the cost of litigation.

Negotiate a Forum Selection Clause.

Sun Tzu, in *The Art of War* (trans. by Thomas Cleary, Shambala Publications, Inc., 1988), points out reasons to avoid fighting long battles deep in foreign territory. The paper war of litigation is no different. If your operations are centered in Seattle, and your counterparty is in Boston, you may be forced to litigate three thousand miles away. In addition to the travel cost and longer absences from your own offices, the legal fees will rise. One solution is to provide in your agreement that any litigation must be brought in your jurisdiction.

In some states, furthermore, the federal district courts may operate more efficiently than local state courts. Elsewhere, the opposite is true. Ask your lawyer whether you have a choice.

Include a Choice of Law Provision.

Different states have different laws. In some multi-state transactions, more than one state's law can arguably govern. The cost of resolving a *choice of law* issue in litigation can be enormous. State in your contract which state's law will apply.

Consider Liquidated Damages.

You can also reduce the cost of litigating and raise the chances of settlement by eliminating fact issues in advance. The most common example is to provide for *liquidated damages*. In some business cases, it costs more to measure actual losses, overhead, and the lost time value of money than it does to prove liability.

With liquidated damages, the parties agree in advance what a breach of the contract will cost. In construction contracts, liquidated damages might be a given amount of money for each day of delay. In a home sale, a defaulting buyer might forfeit the earnest money (or a defaulting seller may return it, doubled). Clauses providing for liquidated damages are generally enforceable if they represent an attempt (however inexact) to value the actual damages caused by default.

Use Business Lawyers to Structure Transactions and Reduce Legal Fees

This chapter is not a *do-it-yourself* kit. The examples are given only to show the need for planning. Except for the most routine transactions, use a business lawyer (See Section Two).

Section Two

AN APPLE A DAY

The message of Section One is that, in law, prevention is cheaper than cure. Section Two describes how to use business lawyers to help you achieve prevention.

Chapter Five explains what business lawyers do and how to find the right one.

Chapter Six discusses the economics of using business lawyers.

Chapter Seven suggests ways to make sure you get the best results from your business lawyer.

Chapter Five

"Good Cholesterol"

For years, cardiologists have warned that cholesterol built up in arteries and shortened lives. More recently, scientists have discovered "good cholesterol" -- a lipoprotein that actually neutralizes "bad" cholesterol and improves health.

Think of business law practice as "good cholesterol." Business lawyers can protect you from litigation. This chapter will explain what to look for in a business lawyer, and how to find one.

1. What to Look for in a Business Lawyer.

Legal advice is valuable only if it comes from the right kind of lawyer. Sometimes you need a specialist. In other situations, you need someone with broader knowledge. In any case, *experience* is critical.

Know when to use a specialist.

The most common specialties (there are several more, with many subspecialties) are:

42

Admiralty	Lending and Banking
Bankruptcy	Media Law
Construction	Oil and Gas
Environmental	Real Estate
Intellectual Property	Securities and Corporate Law
Labor/Employment Law	Tax

In these fields and others, there is no substitute for real expertise. A specialist will probably charge a higher hourly rate, but will work more efficiently on your problem.

Beware of Uncle Sam.

In the regulatory world, the complexity of the law is exploding. Words become more important than facts. As a bar review teacher once put it, "Regulators want to know if you quack like a duck. If you don't quack like a duck, to them you're not a duck."

Informal exchanges with regulators may be good for checking new rules or for discussing hypotheticals. For certainty or for formal proceedings, however, you need a lawyer -- and the lawyer should have experience in the regulatory field in question. Only the right specialist knows how to make you sound like a duck.

Sometimes you need a lawyer with broad knowledge.

For broader questions, you need a generalist. He will know whether you have a problem calling for more specialized advice. A generalist can do for a business client what a point guard does for a basketball team -- he manages the game and gets the ball into the right hands.

Fewer and fewer business lawyers actually call themselves generalists, but a "corporate," "lending," "banking" or "real estate" lawyer usually has broad knowledge.

Shop for experience.

Law school focuses on learning legal concepts and on spotting issues. The typical law school graduate is largely unprepared for solving clients' problems -- that is -- advising them what to do.

Whether a specialist or a generalist, a good lawyer must have more than *knowledge*. He must have *wisdom*. He must understand the practicalities of his advice. It certainly does not hurt if he has some background in your business. For example, the computer engineer who later went to law school is a good candidate to help with your software contract.

2. <u>Finding and Hiring The Business Lawyer</u>.

Use personal recommendations.

Personal references from clients and from other lawyers are invaluable. Ask others in your industry whom they use for particular matters. Make your polling as broad as possible.

Use other professionals to identify lawyers.

Your accountant probably knows a tax lawyer. Maybe your software consultant can recommend a licensing expert. Your banker almost certainly knows several business lawyers. The business lawyer helping you in your home town can easily find a good out-of-town colleague if you need one.

Use bar associations to identify specialists.

Many local bar associations have lawyer-referral services. They can at least give you names of people who hold themselves out as devoting a large part of their practice to a particular field. Some state bar associations can provide a list of certified practitioners. However, a number of laymen have reported problems in getting help from bar associations.

Benefit from seminar contacts.

When you attend seminars, try to meet panelists or attending lawyers. They will usually be thrilled to give you their cards. Business development is one of the reasons they attend.

Use the *Martindale-Hubbell Law Directory*.

If you have no one to recommend a lawyer, or if you want an objective evaluation, use the *Martindale-Hubbell Law Directory*. The directory is published each year in a multi-volume set. It can be found at most law firms, law school libraries, court libraries, and even some public libraries.

Martindale-Hubbell groups all American lawyers by state, city, and firm. Each lawyer prepares his own entry. Each entry gives the lawyer's undergraduate training and law school, and academic honors. The lawyer has an opportunity to identify areas of specialization. If the lawyer clerked for a judge, or has written legal articles or books, the entry will show it.

In a summary section at the front of each volume, *Martindale-Hubbell* also gives separate Legal Ability and General Recommendations ratings. Both ratings are based on confidential surveys of fellow lawyers and judges. The first rating is a measure of expertise -- it can range from "A" (Very High to Preeminent) to "B" (High to Very High) to "C" (Fair to High). The second measure -- the General Recommendation Rating -- addresses ethics, reliability and diligence. It is "pass-fail." If the lawyer does not win a "V" ("Very High"), he will not be rated at all.

Don't rule out a change.

The two most important people you will use outside your firm will be your accountant and your lawyer. Make sure that communication with your lawyer is easy. Make sure that he understands your business and you, and that he has an interest in helping you to succeed.

If you believe that your lawyer is not giving you sound, *constructive*, practical advice, shop around. There are those who can and will. If you have had a bad experience, try another lawyer instead of learning the wrong lesson and staying away from lawyers who can help you keep out of court.

Chapter Six

Home Remedies and the Corner Drug Store

Learning that prevention beats cure is only step one. Step two is learning how to keep prevention costs down. This chapter suggests when and how to seek free or discounted legal advice. This chapter then explores how to maximize the cost-effectiveness of a lawyer when you engage one.

The market for legal services is changing in your favor.

You agree that a front-end investment in legal advice would be wise, but you simply don't have the money now. You think that you have to live with some risk. So far, *the 1990's have not been a seller's market for lawyers.* Take advantage of that fact.

Because there is a glut of lawyers, even traditional *blue-chip* law firms are reconsidering their marketing strategies. If your prospects are good, a shrewd lawyer may see his own gain in befriending a potential new client during its critical early stages of development. You are not limited to *fly-by-nights*, and you lose nothing by asking.

You can often get free or discounted legal advice for simple or routine problems.

A corporate lawyer may help you organize your new venture for little or nothing, in the hope of future business. He may help you at a discount for the sake of the good references you might provide to other potential clients.

You may even convince a good lawyer to take payment in kind. For example, if you run a public relations firm, perhaps you can "pay" the lawyer by giving free advice on the new law firm brochure.

If you have a friend who is a lawyer, or if you already have a lawyer you sometimes use, ask if you can sometimes take him to lunch just to brainstorm about the law that applies to your operations.

Make a lawyer a part of your team.

If your business is a corporation, consider putting a business lawyer on your board of directors. In that role, he can help you spot issues without immediate compensation. If you need deeper involvement from a lawyer, consider giving him a small ownership interest.

To a non-lawyer, this may sound like letting a fox in the hen-house. Clearly, you do not want to let a lawyer (or anyone else) into the inner circle without screening. But generalized feelings that all lawyers are litigation-prone are usually misplaced, especially in the case of business lawyers.

49

Are you ready for in-house counsel?

How much do you budget each year for legal fees and liabilities? If the figure is less than a general counsel's salary -- say, $70,000 to $150,000 -- then you are probably not ready to go "in-house." Another factor pointing to the need for in-house counsel would be a concentration of your legal dealings by geographic area or subject matter. If you know the CEO or counsel for an enterprise which has recently gone "in-house," consider having lunch with one of them. Ask what made them decide to bring a lawyer on staff.

Spend money when you must.

For any important new direction, or for any large transaction, a business lawyer is usually worth hiring. This is true even if you have to borrow to pay him.

Look for opportunities to use lump sum fees.

Chapter Twelve explains how to use hourly and lump sum fees in litigation. Lump sum fees also work in those kinds of transactions that do not involve negotiation. For example, when you incorporate your business, the only players are your lawyer, on the one hand, and you and your advisors, on the other. The same can be true when a lawyer plans the transition of your family business to the next generation. Your lawyer can predict the time he will take. These situations give you a chance to agree with your lawyer in advance how much you will pay. All you need to consider is what will be required of him, and the value of the work to you.

When an hourly fee is necessary, demand estimates and ask for ceilings.

Somewhere in between the perfect world of lump sums and the hurly-burly of litigation fall most negotiations. When you are negotiating with third parties, they usually have a common interest with you in keeping the legal fees of all sides down. However, that interest can sometimes be overridden by their need to see that the contract protects their interests as well as yours. The problem is less acute than in litigation. Still, your counterparty will affect how much time your lawyer spends.

In negotiations, the lawyer is less likely to agree to a lump sum than to give some estimate. These estimates are generally more reliable than for litigation. You can use them to make informed decisions about the economics of going forward. Under certain conditions, you may be able to get the lawyer to commit himself to a ceiling.

Know how soon to involve your business lawyer.

The earlier in your business development that you start a relationship with a business lawyer, the more the attorney is likely to view you as a long-term customer and aggressively seek ways to help you economize.

For particular deals, if you are venturing into strange waters, your business lawyer (particularly in specialized areas) may offer business advice which is worth having at the outset. Otherwise, in routine transactions, or in areas where you have experience, work out the business terms as fully as you can so that the drafting work required of your lawyer is limited.

Make the other side responsible for its negotiating inefficiencies.

Sometimes your lawyer may be drafting the documents, and the other side will only review them. If you have a really difficult counterparty, you may be able to reduce his impact on your legal fees by rewarding him for negotiating efficiently. When you transmit the first draft, for example, you might state:

Enclosed is our first draft. Take as long as you like to review it. Be as thorough as you like. We will try to accommodate all reasonable suggestions. However, after your initial responses are incorporated, we will ask you to pay the legal fees we incur in responding to your suggestions which result from second and third reviews.

This sort of proposal can give offense. Also, it is often hard to separate the time a lawyer spends in smoothing over continuing points of disagreement from the time he spends dealing with new suggestions. Furthermore, as pointed out in Chapter Four, a well-considered document helps to prevent disputes down the road, and to avoid litigation fees that could dwarf your transaction costs.

On the other hand, this tactic may be worth trying if the transaction costs would otherwise make your deal uneconomical. Maybe you can ask your counterparty to *share* the fees you incur as your lawyer responds to his suggestions, especially after the first round. However, if your counterparty does share some of the cost of your lawyer, take care to specify *in writing* to your counterparty that you, and not the counterparty, are your lawyer's client.

You can use business lawyers cost-effectively.

The secret to using business lawyers is to know what you need. Ask how you can best fill that need at the least cost. Answering these questions will become easier with practice.

Chapter Seven

A Spoonful of Sugar

The word "lawyer" is slowly becoming a verb. More and more books and articles on practice management and client development speak of "the art of lawyering" and of "lawyering skills." Clients need the same kind of advice on their side. This chapter explores the "art of clienting" and "clienting skills." It discusses what to expect from business lawyers and how to prevent deal-killing.

1. What to Expect from a Business Lawyer.

Quite simply, what you get from a business lawyer depends on what you need and on what you can pay.

For certainty, consider a regulatory business review letter.

Many regulatory agencies will give a business review letter agreeing (or disagreeing) that a proposal conforms to applicable law. A lawyer should act as your middleman. The process is usually expensive.

Get opinion letters for maximum comfort (but not for certainty).

For most people, receiving an opinion letter is as close as you will ever come to "going all the way" with a business lawyer. In an opinion letter, the firm states that, based on certain documents, facts and assumptions, a certain conclusion is true: that your video store is not violating the Americans with Disabilities Act; or that your restrictive licensing agreement would survive antitrust challenge and is enforceable according to its terms. Here is an example of an unqualified opinion:

> *Dear John:*
>
> *We have examined all documents and obtained all information that we think is necessary for the rendering of this opinion. It is our opinion that none of your operations, present or planned, raises any question regarding compliance with any applicable law or regulations.*
>
> *Sincerely,*
>
> *Perry*

You will never receive an opinion letter similar to this. They will all contain one or more of the following (or other) qualifications:

- Issues examined: "You have asked for our opinion as to the validity and enforceability of the proposed sale agreement . . . ."

- Information reviewed: "We have reviewed the articles of incorporation and by-laws of your company and the proposed sale agreement . . . ."

o   Areas of competence: "We are lawyers licensed to practice in the State of Rhode Island and express no opinion as to the law of any other state . . . ."

o   Exceptions to opinion: "It is our opinion that the sale agreement is valid and enforceable according to its terms, *subject to the law of bankruptcy* . . . ."

As you increase your sophistication, you can bargain with your business lawyer by negotiating qualifications and disclaimers. Discuss the "carve-outs" with your lawyer to make sure they do not affect the essential value of the opinion.

o   Should we have asked for your opinion on more than this issue?

o   Is there additional information you did not review that might affect your opinion?

o   Is there any other state's law that might be important? Does it justify getting a subsidiary opinion from counsel in that state?

o   What *are* the dangers if the other side goes bankrupt? What relief would be available?

Confirm these discussions in writing, even if only in an informal letter written by you. If a lawyer cannot explain a "carve-out" or stand behind his explanation, he may not have the expertise you thought you bargained for.

Many business deals today have important tax effects. Make sure your lawyer knows whether you are relying on him to spot tax issues in connection with the work he is doing.

An opinion is not a guarantee.

In an opinion letter, the lawyer is liable to you only for negligence. If the law is unclear or changing, a "wrong" opinion may not be negligent.

From opinion letters, the only way is down.

Every other dealing between a client and a business lawyer is a kind of cheaper and less meaningful alternative to an opinion letter. Close to an opinion letter is a memorandum outlining a firm's research on a given question. Such a memorandum may state that it is not an opinion, but the author may give you some range of the risks of liability.

In an example further down the totem pole, the writer of another "how-to" book faced the prospect of paying $1,500 to $3,000 for an opinion that his book did not infringe any copyright or defame anyone. Instead, the author asked a media lawyer to mark those parts of the work that raised any concern. The items found were not integral to the work, and the author simply deleted them, rather than pay for more research. As a result, the media lawyer's fee was only $300.

At the lowest end of the scale is the curbside advice discussed in Chapter Six, where, as the saying goes, "you get what you pay for."

Tailor the work to fit your economics.

For ongoing operations, the happiest medium may be to consult with a business lawyer on a paid basis as you develop your business, so that you are getting the benefit of his wisdom as you go, without the disclaimers and cost of a more formal exchange such as an opinion letter. When certainty is needed, you can discuss the issue and the cost of resolving it. Depending on the cost, you can either ask for an opinion letter or change your plans to avoid the issue.

2. Prevent Unnecessary "Deal-Killing."

A common objection to using lawyers is that they are "deal-killers." In their defense, some deals *need* killing. Often, when a lawyer has "killed" your deal, all he has done is foresee an unsolvable problem.

On the other hand, some lawyers kill deals unnecessarily. Knowing some realities about lawyers will help you understand this problem and avoid it.

The incentives in legal practice are toward mistake avoidance.

Business lawyers are terribly afraid of risking a mistake. Mistakes often cause concrete injuries which any client can clearly see. On the other hand, only the most perceptive client knows when a job is unusually well done; and only the rarest gives a direct reward. It should not be surprising that the professional sitting across the desk from you is prone to be careful. If your deal is complex or poses substantial risks, he may counsel against it altogether. In his experience, that may seem safer than trying to lead you through the brambles.

Don't be offended if you find yourself *selling* the deal to your lawyer, so that he fully understands its opportunities, and the risks you are willing to assume. This is not to suggest that you talk your lawyer out of doing his job. The point is to prevent the "killing" of deals through poor communication.

Communicate thoroughly.

If you give your lawyer bad information you will get a bad product. This is another reason why your knowledge is important. The more you know, the more sensitive you will be to his need for information. When your lawyer requests data from you, try not to sit on the request or shuffle it off to someone who lacks the knowledge to respond.

Communicate ends, rather than means.

Be conscious of how you communicate. Describe your *strategy* to your lawyer. Let him recommend *tactics*. Instead of telling your lawyer *what* you want, tell him *why* you want it. Even if your original conception won't fly, he may think of an alternative that you might have preferred in the first place, if it had occurred to you.

"Deal-killing" can reflect a lack of confidence.

Deal-killing can also result when a lawyer is unfamiliar with your field. One who is sure-footed on your terrain is more comfortable trying some acrobatics.

Most business lawyers are "left-brain" thinkers.

Another reason business lawyers sometimes "kill" deals is based on their natural thinking preferences. Scientists know that the left hemisphere of the brain deals with analytical and quantitative thinking; the right hemisphere handles the intuitive and creative. Although everyone is capable of thinking in either hemisphere, different people show marked preferences. These preferences correlate with certain occupations. Right-brain thinkers tend to become architects, artists and entrepreneurs. Left-brain thinkers are attracted to administration, accounting and (you guessed it) law.

Left-brain thinkers view creative ideas with suspicion. When your right-brain idea goes under the microscope of your left-brain lawyer, he sees the flaws, the risks, the imperfections. He is unlikely to see as clearly as you do the opportunities.

Perhaps you will stumble across a right-brain lawyer. Though rare, they do exist. The right-brain lawyer knows how to use his left-brain colleagues for feedback. He knows how to use their knowledge to take you in the right direction, rather than to kill your deal.

Maybe you do not need a right-brain lawyer. Maybe you are so creative that you need a nay-sayer for balance. Maybe you have a left-brain preference yourself and would be turned off by a lawyer who thinks differently. If so, you certainly have more to choose from. Furthermore, many left-brain lawyers are sensitive to criticisms of deal-killing. They strain to balance their natural suspicion with optimism. Many have even learned at seminars how to deal with clients like you. So if you have trouble telling left from right, all may not be lost.

Dr. Yes and Dr. No

A colleague tells the story of a client who uses two different tax lawyers. One of these tax lawyers he calls "Dr. Yes." The other is "Dr. No." When the client wants to accept a deal, he sends it to Dr. Yes. When he wants to reject an offer and needs an excuse, he relies on Dr. No. He is mastering the art of "clienting."

Section Three

DAMAGE CONTROL

Disputes need not turn into litigation. Section Three examines three ways of keeping disputes under control.

Chapter Eight explains the economics of settlement, and suggests some approaches to settling.

Chapter Nine outlines how to use *alternative methods of dispute resolution,* such as arbitration and mediation, with less cost and delay than litigation.

Chapter Ten suggests how and when to get governmental enforcement authorities to press claims for you.

Chapter Eight

Settle!

Many lawyers are familiar with the advice Abraham Lincoln (a lawyer) gave to colleagues: "Discourage litigation. Persuade your neighbors to compromise whenever you can. Point out to them how the nominal winner is often a real loser -- in fees, expenses, and waste of time."

The four steps to settling.

o Do the arithmetic.

o Overcome any bias against settling.

o Get the personalities out of the way.

o Negotiate effectively.

1. <u>Do the Arithmetic.</u>

Assume that your customer claims $20,000. Assume that you have some arguable defenses, and that your chances of defeating the claim are fifty percent. Multiplying the total claim ($20,000) times your chances of winning (fifty percent) gives you an average or projected loss value of $10,000.

It would be hard to defend the case for less than $10,000. Thus, if you litigate, you will have costs above $10,000, *on top of* your projected liability of $10,000. This amount is greater than the claim.

Your state may also require you to pay legal interest on the claim, while it is pending, at a rate higher than inflation. The legal interest will probably exceed the return you could get on your money by investing it. If you lose, you may even have to pay your opponent's attorneys fees. Thus, the economics of defending a small to mid-sized claim are often poor. Furthermore, none of this takes into account the time you will spend giving information to your lawyer, and preparing for and attending depositions and trial.

None of these additional losses come into play if you settle early. In the example, you would be better off swallowing your pride and writing a check for the $20,000 originally claimed.

For too many businesses, the pattern is the same: the demand letter is ignored; suit is filed; a litigator is hired. Before long, the attorney has billed $7,000. He projects future costs of $6,000 more. He tells the client that the chances of success are roughly even. Only now does the client begin to think about trying to settle. Under the earlier example, if the plaintiff is still willing to negotiate, after being forced to incur substantial legal fees, the defendant would be very lucky to settle for $10,000.

Certainly litigation has its place. The economics would change if the size of the claim increased to $200,000.

Litigating a $200,000 case usually costs more than a $20,000 one, but not ten times more. It might be economical to invest $40,000 in defending a $200,000 claim, where investing $10,000 to defend a $20,000 claim would be a losing proposition.

Before you automatically begin a defense, investigate the claim. If a claim involves a particular employee, interview others besides him. Check with the employees who work most closely with him, too. Use in-house people if you have them, or your litigator if you do not.

Base your decision whether to settle on cold-blooded math and full information.

2. Overcome Any Bias Against Settling.

Be conscious of your own bias in settling.

Are you sure that you can see your dispute neutrally? A common adage among litigators is that if both parties to a settlement are unhappy, it is probably a good settlement. This means that both sides have probably overcome their instinctive favoritism for their own position.

Know when deterrence is a consideration and when it is not.

In some cases deterrence considerations come into play. If your opponent knows his claim is weak, but sues you to get a quick settlement, there may be a danger of starting a trend. Will others learn of your opponent's success and follow his lead? If so, it might be in your long-term interest to invest even $30,000 to defeat a $20,000 demand. If deterrence is a part of your settlement policy, then give it maximum effect by advertising it. Make sure your employees, for example, learn of it before the first one sues you.

Deterrence may be important if you defend suits frequently. In some cases, however, the decision is almost knee-jerk. Some businesses seem to have a stated or unstated policy of simply making life miserable for anyone who sues them. The decision is made without considering how it will really affect other potential litigants. Unless you get a real benefit from litigating, try to overcome the instinctive resistance to settling, or the feeling that it is caving in.

Don't kill the messenger.

Lawyers who try to settle cases are sometimes viewed as weak. "I want a fighter on my side," you say. Certainly, you must have a litigator who knows how to get a judgment in your favor. But there is no correlation between a lawyer's capacity to fight effectively and his questioning whether doing so is in your best interest.

In *Gone With the Wind,* the Southern planters celebrate the coming of war with little anticipation of the waste and frustration to come. The modern-day warrior who most welcomes a chance to litigate is often the one to react the most angrily when he learns the realities.

3. <u>Get the Personalities Out of the Way.</u>

Paying a doubtful claim in full is sometimes wiser than fighting it. In most cases, however, payment in full would probably not be necessary. A prompt response and a word of sympathy may put you in a position to settle for less than the claim.

Dear John:

I was sorry to learn that you lost a sale while your telephone system was inoperable. You are one of our most valued customers, and we want to make your telephone system as reliable as possible.

In this particular case, there is some evidence that your building power failed. We have found it very unusual for this particular system to break down unless there is a power failure. Another one of our purchasers in your building complained of a power failure that same day.

We would also point out that your demand letter claims the full gross price for the sale you lost. In our previous conversations, you advised that your direct expenses on sales average thirty percent.

We are less interested in quarreling about these issues at mutual expense than we are in maintaining our very good relationship with you. If you are

---

agreeable to our proposal, we would like to send you $10,000 worth of back-up equipment as compensation for your loss.

Sincerely,

John Doe

Note that, in the letter, the writer does not admit fault or sacrifice his position in the event that litigation should become necessary (Also look for ways to substitute "in-kind" payments for cash).

Show your proposed letter to a lawyer. Get his advice on how to reserve your rights to contest the claim, without hurting your goal of conciliation. *Compared to the cost of litigating, these are legal fees well spent.*

Understand the positive impact of personal conversations.

It is usually good to preface your letter with a telephone call. The call should have the same tone as the letter. Show sympathy without conceding liability. Promise a letter outlining what you plan to do (keep your promise and send the letter promptly). To show even deeper commitment on your part, set up a face-to-face meeting.

Beware of individuals likely to block settlement.

Even good settlement tactics can fail because of personality conflicts. Maybe the personality problem is yours; maybe it is your employee's; maybe it is an employee of the other side. Here are some suggestions.

When you are the problem, replace yourself.

Look, Elizabeth, I really think Suitprone is jerking me around. When I gave them an estimate, I told them it was only an estimate. Now they are saying they never would have authorized the work if they had known it would cost this much. But I was on the phone with them through the whole process. They knew exactly how much work I was doing.

Anyway, it's hard for me to discuss this without getting angry. Can you try to work something out with Suitprone? I think you will be able to approach it more calmly. I will authorize whatever you can work out.

Winston Churchill said that defeat, no matter how you rationalize or explain it, is always bitter. Even when your settlement papers proclaim that they are not an admission of liability, settling can make you feel that your personal actions have been questioned. It is natural to resist. Find someone else to resolve the conflict -- someone with your best interests at heart, but with no previous actions to justify.

When your employee is the problem, replace him.

Look, Jim, Suitprone is upset about the bill for $10,000. They say that it's three times higher than the estimate.

It's clear to me that you were not doing unnecessary work. And based on what you have told me, I think the Suitprone people were naive not to realize that this was taking more of your time than you originally projected. I do think that because of the personalities involved, I want Bill, rather than you, to negotiate some compromise with Suitprone. I am doing this only to save time and expense. I find no fault with you whatsoever. In fact, giving up the Suitprone account will give you more time to handle our new account with General Motors.

Encourage your employees to tell you when friction is developing. The earlier they tell you, the better. This will happen only if they believe that you will not penalize them.

When the other side's employee is the problem, consider going around him.

Hello, Sarah. This is John Doe calling. Listen, we still have an outstanding receivable for $10,000 from Suitprone. Frank in your office is upset because the bill tripled the estimate. That is a big difference, but Jim was handling the account. You know from experience that he never does any unnecessary work. Also, Jim was in touch with Frank through the whole *process. Frank really should not have been surprised by the amount.*

I have a proposal. Let's reduce the invoice to $8,000. For the future, we will send you written interim statements so that none of your managers will be surprised at the amount after completion. When you tell Frank what you settled for, you can also tell him that because of his watchfulness, you are insisting on a new system of interim statements from us.

Bypassing a manager may meet resistance from his superior, and can work only if your relationship is already strong. Try a switch at your end first. When you do go around the other side's employee, do whatever you can to mollify the person bypassed. He can often be in a position to affect future business. Weigh the possible harm from offending him against the stakes of the present disagreement.

4. <u>Negotiate Effectively</u>.

Roger Fisher and William Ury have written a book titled *Getting to Yes: Negotiating Agreements Without Giving In* (Rev. ed., Viking-Penguin 1991). It provides an excellent and very readable set of general rules for negotiating. There really is no substitute for reading it.

Here are some other suggestions peculiar to settling legal claims.

Settle quickly if you can.

It is often easier to settle early. The longer you delay, the more you risk recharging the other side's emotional batteries. Also, after your counterparty has paid attorneys fees, he may lose interest in settling. If you miss critical chances to settle early, an interest in settlement may not reemerge until you are "on the courthouse steps." By then, you will have made a substantial investment.

Know when to involve a lawyer in settlement.

Lawyers can help when you need a case analysis to decide how much to offer. Lawyers can also help to move a stubborn opponent. They can certainly help in advising how to make sure your settlement document prevents future lawsuits.

On the other hand, some lawyers can get in the way. Most lawyers are far-sighted enough to know that they benefit from helping you, but some *may be* affected by the loss of a fee generator, even if unconsciously. This is not usually a problem where you already have a good relationship with a lawyer. But if you have these concerns about a lawyer who has helped you for a long time, you may need to switch.

Other lawyers sometimes delay settlement to make sure they have done enough investigation. Often, this process lasts too long.

Here are some considerations:

1. If your relationship with the "adversary" is friendly and open, and the conflict involves mainly business issues, try to keep direct channels of communication open.

2. If legal issues predominate, but the business relationship is good, consider making the lawyer an equal partner in your negotiations.

3. If there is a personality conflict that cannot be cured, communication through lawyers *may* improve the chances of settlement.

4. You should also use a lawyer when you have a claim with no genuine dispute, but the other side is stalling and is an individual or small operation who can be intimidated by a letter on a lawyer's stationery.

If you can't settle all, settle some.

If you cannot settle the case, you might agree to a partial settlement:

o Perhaps you can admit that you were at fault, and agree that the only issue is the amount of the damages.

o   Perhaps you can settle for all out-of-pocket losses, and agree that the only issue is the claim for lost profits.

o   Perhaps you can agree on the total amount of the loss, but litigate who was at fault.

If you cannot reach even a partial settlement, at least stipulate as many facts as you can. Give the litigators as little as possible to fight over.

Chapter Nine

Arbitrate. Mediate.
Toss a Coin.

Now is the great moment. For two years, you have spent hours each week working with your lawyer to get the case ready for trial. You have paid a pretty penny, and you know that the billing for this last month of trial preparation will be enormous. But it's worth it. The defendant will finally have to explain to a jury why it stole your idea. Your witnesses from all over the country are landing one-by-one at the airport like avenging angels.

Your lawyer emerges from the final pretrial meeting with the judge. You can tell he has bad news. "I'm afraid we've been bumped," he says. "The judge has decided to hear a different case instead of ours. We'll try again next September."

The court system can frustrate even the most cost-conscious litigators. As a result, more and more lawyers and sophisticated clients are turning to *alternative methods of dispute resolution,* or *ADR's. Arbitration* and *mediation* are the best-known examples. This chapter discusses the following:

o   Arbitration, mediation, and related dispute resolution services;

o   How to use arbitration;

o   Procedural considerations; and

o   How to get more information.

1. ADR's and Other Dispute Resolution Services

Arbitration

In arbitration, both sides present their case to a panel of *arbitrators* (usually three, but one is not unheard of). The parties can agree in advance that the decision of the panel will have the same binding effect as a court judgment.

The arbitrators often have specialized knowledge. For example, the panel for a construction dispute might well consist of architects or engineers. This can be important in a case involving technology or complex fact issues. Presenting such a case to a jury, or even to a judge with no experience in the field, makes the outcome less predictable. Also, the cost of presenting a complex issue to lay people can be enormous. They may not understand commonly used industry terms. Expensive "demonstrative" evidence may be necessary. Arbitrators, on the other hand, although you will have to pay them, are usually "singing from your sheet of music." They also work more around *your* schedule.

The law is generally not binding on the arbitrators. Instead, arbitrators use the law more for guidance and to help decide what the parties had in mind in negotiating or performing their contract. For this reason, arbitration usually brings less opportunity for expensive research and briefing. The rules of evidence do not strictly apply, so the presentation of facts is generally easier, faster and cheaper than in court trials. Also, the right to appeal an arbitration award is extremely limited.

Mediation and mini-trials

Mediation is less formal than arbitration. Here, the parties select a neutral mediator -- often a retired judge. Depending on the agreement between the parties, the mediator can either render a binding decision, or merely serve as a facilitator for settlement. Usually, the parties make the process non-binding. As with arbitration, mediation lets you pick your own fact-finder. You can present the case with fewer procedural constraints. As in arbitration, you can usually avoid the costs of appeal.

A *mini-trial* is a variation where the parties, advised by a neutral mediator, hear presentations from their own and opposing counsel, then try to settle.

Pros and cons of arbitration and mediation

Not everyone likes arbitration and mediation. Some lawyers bring the sort of contentious tactics to arbitration that its efficiencies are lost. Also, because appeals are not usually available, there is little relief from a bad result.

Non-binding mediation can be a waste of time if your opponent will not listen to your arguments, or is not seriously interested in settlement.

There really is no kind of case which cannot be arbitrated, as long as the parties agree. Again, a complex or technological case is the kind which calls for arbitration the loudest. If your case is weak, and a confused jury is your only hope, you may think twice about arbitration. A more legitimate reason not to submit to arbitration would be where the letter of the law is squarely on your side. If you have relied on the letter of the law in structuring your deal, you might feel cheated if an arbitration panel chose some middle-of-the-road solution.

In a different case, a colleague asked for a jury trial when a credit agreement was vague and could be construed several ways, but an out-of-town lender had acted in bad faith. Here, the borrower clearly benefitted from the use of a jury in his home town.

When you have this kind of advantage making it unwise for you to submit to arbitration, use your advantage for leverage in settlement negotiations.

"Splitting the baby."

Critics of arbitration charge that arbitrators tend to avoid hard choices, and "split the baby" instead. To rebut that criticism, the American Arbitration Association surveyed all of its commercial arbitration awards rendered from January through December of 1991. According to

AAA figures, fewer than one out of eight awards fell between forty and fifty-nine percent of the claim. Nearly one out of four fell in the ranges of twenty to thirty-nine percent or sixty to seventy-nine percent of the claim. In nearly two-thirds of the cases, the awards reflected clear winners: the arbitrators either denied the claim, allowed less than nineteen percent of the claim, or awarded over eighty percent of the claim. If these figures are representative, then concerns about "splitting the baby" would seem overstated or outdated.

Alternative dispute resolution services.

More and more corporations and counsel are moving to make arbitration more common. In the early 1980's, a number of national corporations joined to form the Center for Public Resources. The Center aggressively promotes ADR's. In an article in the November 4, 1991, edition of the *Cincinnati Business Courier*, the Center's president, James Henry, estimated that members of the Center had saved more than $100 million in legal costs through ADR's.

The American Arbitration Association and its regional offices offer panelists and rules for those wishing to use arbitration. A list of these offices is provided at the end of this book as Appendix 1. The International Chamber of Commerce, headquartered in Paris, offers arbitration services for international business disputes.

Most major cities have private mediation services. Simply check the heading "Mediation Service(s)" in the Yellow Pages.

2. How to Use Arbitration or Mediation

Consider putting an arbitration clause in your agreement. An arbitration clause gives either party the right to insist on arbitration when the other side sues. The American Arbitration Association suggests the following standard clause:

Any controversy or claim arising out of or relating to this contract, or the breach thereof, shall be settled by arbitration in accordance with the Commercial Arbitration Rules of the American Arbitration Association, and judgment upon the award rendered by the arbitrator(s) may be entered in any court having jurisdiction thereof.

Arbitration by demand.

If your agreement has an arbitration clause, either side may unilaterally demand arbitration. The American Arbitration Association also provides a standard form for this purpose.

Arbitration by submission.

If there is no binding agreement to arbitrate, then both parties must jointly seek arbitration. This process is called a *submission*. Again, the American Arbitration Association can provide a standardized form. A checklist for initiating arbitration through the AAA appears at Appendix 2.

3. Procedural Considerations for Arbitration

To increase the time and cost savings of arbitration, do some planning in the transacting stage. For example, an arbitration clause should specify in advance where the arbitration will take place.

Plan ahead for the selection of arbitrators.

The arbitration clause can specifically identify the arbitrator(s). If not, it can name a selection process or qualifications.

Set the boundaries of any disputes.

The arbitration clause can limit the issues to be tried, or the relief given. For example, the parties can partially "settle" a case by agreeing in advance that if one party is found liable, the damages will fall within a certain range.

Know the alternatives for provisional remedies.

One concern about arbitration is the unavailability of *provisional remedies*: court orders that protect a litigant while a case is proceeding. For example, *injunctions* forbid parties from doing anything to change the current state of affairs until the case is decided. *Writs of attachment* or *sequestration* forbid the debtor from disposing of assets.

By the submission form or in the contractual arbitration clause, the parties can empower the arbitrators to grant

81

provisional relief. Alternatively, the agreement can provide that either party can seek provisional relief from a court.

4. How to Get More Information

A list of American Arbitration offices appears at the end of this book as Appendix 1. A list of publications giving more information about ADR's appears as Appendix 3.

Arbitration is Used too Seldom.

It is perplexing that ADR's are not more widespread. Litigators sometimes discourage it because of a sense that it does not allow them to do as thorough a job. Some quite scrupulous litigators want to unearth the truth (or brief a legal issue to the point of metaphysical certainty), regardless of cost. Even when you share your litigator's concern for exhaustive discovery or research, you can agree in an arbitration clause or in a submission to allow full discovery or to apply the law literally. If your lawyer gives you a convincing argument against arbitration (they do exist in individual cases), by all means, listen to him. But if he has had a bad experience in arbitration, ask him if the problem could not be cured by selecting a better panel. Ask him also if his concern is something that can be solved by a thoughtfully drafted arbitration clause or submission paper.

Litigation also seems to have a kind of "high noon" mystique. Arbitration just doesn't get your adrenalin going the way a good trial does. But if you just want some notches in your gun, get them by having a more profitable year than your competitor, rather than by insisting on your day in court.

Chapter Ten

Call the Cops

That competitor of yours has been undercutting you for a year. Now you know why. You just hired their former vice-president, and he tells you the whole story. They have been in gross violation of the same regulations you spent a fortune to obey. The only trouble is, your business is getting by on a shoestring. You can hardly afford to pay a Washington lawyer to sue for regulatory violations. Who knows if you have any right to sue anyway?

You don't always have to be your own gunslinger. When someone has committed a crime against you, know when to use a criminal referral. When a competitor has an advantage because he is ignoring regulations you obey, know when and how to alert regulatory agencies. This chapter explains how and when to use governmental enforcement authorities to press your claims for you.

1. Consider Criminal Referrals When You are the Victim of a Crime

Whenever you are the victim of a crime, you probably have civil remedies. For example, if your employee embezzles from you, you can sue him for reimbursement. However, the economics may not favor taking action. Perhaps the chances of collecting are slim. Or the cost of suing is out of proportion to the loss. For cases such as these, consider criminal referrals. If the prosecutors get a conviction, one of the available remedies is restitution. The service is free to you.

There are some limitations.

Restitution orders are often only partial. You also have no control over the proceedings. Prosecutors may not give the case the same priority you would. Once begun, most criminal investigations are confidential. You may not even know what the prosecutors are doing.

If there is an indictment, of course, you may have to spend some time giving evidence. Also, think twice about referring someone for prosecution if there is already a good chance of a "friendly" resolution or collection. A criminal prosecution may destroy his capacity to pay you and kill any hope of collecting.

WARNING: Never, never, never <u>threaten</u> anyone with a criminal prosecution.

It is a crime to threaten someone with a criminal referral to obtain any kind of advantage (such as to get a civil settlement). The crime is extortion. The only safe way to do a criminal referral is simply to do it. Don't talk about doing it.

Also be conscious of the laws of defamation and malicious prosecution. You are not liable merely because the defendant is found innocent. But make sure you have a reasonable basis for making the referral.

If this sounds like a long list of negatives, it is. Criminal referrals are a remedy of last resort. But if nothing else is available, don't rule them out.

2. When Another Business Injures You by Violating The Law, Consider Notifying Regulators.

Regulatory violations can injure you in two different ways. They may injure you directly: perhaps your suppliers are "price-fixing" in violation of antitrust laws; perhaps you are a victim of bid-rigging; perhaps someone sells you an investment without disclosing material facts.

Competitors may also harm you indirectly -- by ignoring the same rules you spend money to follow: maybe another shipper isn't filing tariffs; maybe the distributor across town is ignoring environmental regulations. These violations can put your competitor in a position to undercut your prices.

Whether your injury is direct or indirect, consider making a referral.

If you find yourself in one of these situations, ask a lawyer if there is some agency with authority to enforce compliance. Private complaints are the reason the Antitrust Division of the Justice Department begins most of its investigations. The most common reports are the complaints of bid-rigging by failed bidders, or of price-fixing by a customer who thinks all of his suppliers are in collusion. If an agency takes action, "equitable disgorgement" or restitution may be awarded to those directly injured. Even when you have not been directly injured, and therefore do not receive compensation, a competitor may at least lose an unfair advantage.

Most federal agencies, including the Environmental Protection Agency, the Justice Department and the Securities and Exchange Commission, will act on anonymous complaints. State and local equivalents often do, too.

Agency referrals have limitations, too.

Some agencies often get "crank" calls. They will give priority to those claims that offer the most credible presentations. Enclose documents, if available. As with ordinary criminal proceedings, you have no control over the investigation. You will probably not be kept advised. Even when the agency pursues your claim, it will take time.

Match the procedure to your goal.

The most common methods of reporting are telephone calls. Anonymous letters or simple packages of incriminating documents rank second and third. With the first method -- telephone calls -- it may be difficult to remain anonymous. Once the agency knows your identity, you are likely to be called to give evidence. If you are in doubt, ask a lawyer what procedure to follow to assure that you remain anonymous. Many agencies will allow a law firm to give the information without identifying the client.

Referrals are a last resort.

Criminal and regulatory referrals seldom give you slam-dunk victories. If mishandled, they can get you into trouble. Use them when the *status quo* is intolerable, but when litigation does not make sense.

Section Four

WAR!

Your secretary hands you an envelope from that prestigious law firm you recently hired. The plaintiff, Suitprone, has threatened to take you to the cleaners, but you are in good hands. Your lawyers are a bulwark against the impending raid on your treasury. You open the envelope and examine their statement for the first month of services.

The amount seems a little steep: $6000 for preparing your initial pleadings, sending some written discovery, and reviewing your files? At this rate, the fees may eventually exceed the claim. And who are all these people putting time on your file? You met the partner and one associate at the initial interview. Who are these other people doing research and drafting pleadings?

And look at this entry by the partner for answering your secretary's telephone call just to confirm that your FAX arrived. One quarter of an hour? At $175 per hour? That comes to $43.75 for a minute on the telephone!

Look at these cost items: 25¢ per page for the copies of your files? Overtime for the secretary who stayed late on your case? Pizza for the associates who stayed after hours to finish your pleadings in time? You begin to wonder whether you need to be as careful with your law firm as with Suitprone.

Probably not. Despite the mistrust with which much of the business community regards lawyers, hardly any are actually "out to get you." Litigation costs are out of control largely because our adversarial system is not a business-like way to resolve disputes. If this surprises you, try arbitration a few times. If you use lawyers who believe in arbitration, and pick good arbitrators, you will probably save more litigation dollars than by "legal audits" or any other monitoring techniques.

The lawyers who do "pad bills" or knowingly do unnecessary work are certainly to be avoided, but they are only a small part of the problem. A more common danger is the lawyer who is focused so exclusively on winning your case that he forgets to "think like a client."

Section Four tells you what the most common problems are and how to address them in a businesslike way.

Chapter Eleven

Finding a General

Even inside the air-conditioned courtroom, it is hot. Your lawyer reads from his notes. Without looking up, he asks the next question. The witness answers. Your lawyer ignores him. He is already looking for the next question. He reads again.

The jurors have blank expressions. Some look down. Mostly, their eyes wander over the courtroom walls. They are a million miles away. The judge examines routine papers delivered to him by the clerk. Your lawyer drones on forever. You can tell the case is being lost before your eyes.

Remember, litigation is war. When you wage war, you need a general. Actually, a good litigator is not only a general, but also a writer, an actor, and a symphony conductor as well. A litigator is a specialist. You need to know how to recognize this person and where to look.

1. The Criteria for Choosing a Litigator

You want a litigator who maximizes your chances of winning. The larger the amount in dispute, the more important skill becomes, compared to the cost of litigating. Only in small suits, or suits of doubtful collectibility, is cost as important as skill.

How a litigator affects your chances of winning.

Statistics from jury polls show that in eighty percent of all jury trials, the jury verdict merely confirms tentative conclusions *which the jury has reached before the end of the lawyers' opening statements.* Think about that. Four times out of five, the jury has decided your case before it has heard you or any other witness speak a word. The jurors have based their thinking on the opening statements of the lawyers alone. Of course, your litigator must build upon the facts which you dumped into his lap. He cannot recreate them. But he must persuade the jury that his interpretation of the facts is best.

How to judge the cost of a litigator.

After skill, cost is next in importance. And cost cannot be determined by numbers alone. A litigator with an hourly rate of $150 may, by his greater experience, be able to prepare a case better and for a lower total cost than someone billing $120 per hour.

A litigator should be able to help you judge the cost of litigating.

You also need someone who can communicate the possible outcomes and their economic impact. You need someone who can accurately judge whether you can settle now on better terms than the projected net outcome of going forward. You may also need recommendations whether certain items of work are justified in terms of how much they increase the chances of winning.

Unfortunately, not every skillful trial lawyer is good at this kind of analysis. A previous chapter argued that most business lawyers are "left-brain" thinkers. Many jury trial lawyers are an exception. The courtroom wizard who has the perfect sense of how far to go in cross-examination may be less adept in answering your questions about numbers. In many cases, this problem diminishes with age. Even if he does not use mathematical terms, a more experienced litigator may have reliable economic instincts.

2. How to Find a Litigator.

If you were forced to bet $500,000--or your business--on a match-up between two athletes, you would surely do a little homework before choosing. You would probably read sports magazines and consult your most knowledgeable friends. You would hope to interview coaches, scouts, or other players. You might even ask for game film. In choosing a litigator for the same stakes, however, too many people take the first suggestion they get.

If you follow the advice given in previous chapters, you will establish a relationship with a business lawyer before you need a litigator. For technical cases that involve mainly questions of law, the business lawyer may be right for the job. For cases which require a good knowledge of litigation procedure, or agility in the courtroom, you need a litigation specialist.

Don't wait to identify a litigator until you need one.

Why compress your time for making such an important decision? For routine cases, develop a relationship with a litigator before you need one. This litigator can also speed up the search for a specialist when you do need one.

Your business lawyer can help you find a litigator.

Your business lawyer may have a partner, associate, or friend who is a good litigator. If so, your business lawyer can serve as a translator when necessary and help you monitor the economics of the case. Particularly if the business lawyer uses someone at his own firm, he may even reserve the authority to review your bills before they are sent.

Be careful, however, where your business lawyer is only an associate at his firm and refers you to a litigation partner at the same firm. He may have little control over the litigator. Your status as a client may be less than if you had found a litigator at another firm. Set the same ground rules you would otherwise set. Deal directly with the partner, even if the firm designates you on its records as the associate's client.

To locate out-of-town counsel, or in the event of a conflict, perhaps a litigator at your business lawyer's firm can recommend someone. Litigators interact more often than business lawyers do, so you should have a wider range of references.

Other ways to locate a litigator.

If you do not have a business lawyer to guide you to a litigator, ask around. Which litigators do similar companies use? Go further than getting a name. Did they find the lawyer effective? How did his rates compare to the amount in dispute? How well were they able to communicate with him?

Publications such as the *Martindale-Hubbell* directory, discussed in Chapter Five for business lawyers, apply to litigators as well.

Interview the candidates.

Once you have a few different candidates, interview them.

o   Ask each one for his experience with problems similar to yours.

o   Ask for an elementary analysis of your case.

o   Ask for a proposal on fees.

o   Ask if there would be a conflict of interest in representing you, based on the identity of the other parties to the case.

o   Ask anything you genuinely would like to know.

Interviews accomplish two things. First, you can learn which lawyer makes you the most comfortable. Although you are not interviewing him for membership in a social club, you certainly do want someone who does not make communicating feel like a chore.

Second, when the lawyer knows that you are shopping around, his perception of you and the desirability of your case may improve. This may make him somewhat more willing to negotiate on fees and, if you are a new client, on how much to demand as a deposit.

Litigators are not fungible.

There are vast differences in the skills of litigators. Even highly credentialed lawyers may do poorly in court. Some lawyers who consider themselves experienced *litigators* may prepare excellent pleadings, but tremble at the courtroom door. Hiring a litigator is a high risk investment. Finding the right one is worth the effort.

Chapter Twelve

Soldier's Pay

Bill is a fifth-year associate. Soon he will be considered for partner. Now, more than ever, he must be sure his billable hours do not sag. He knows that his firm attracts clients by offering low hourly rates. Associates are expected to make up the difference by working files thoroughly. Each associate is budgeted to bill 2,300 hours per year.

For whatever reason, work has been a little slow. The only big case that is active at the moment is that products liability claim. Right now, there are no depositions scheduled. No pleadings need filing. This might be a good time just to call the lawyer for one of the co-defendants to see what he is thinking about the case.

"Hello, David." "Hello, Bill." After five minutes of shooting the breeze about the NBA playoffs, Bill confirms what he suspected: David agrees that the plaintiff, Suitprone, is way off base. There was obviously contributory negligence. And if any defendant is liable, it's not Bill or David's client. Five more minutes on the playoffs.

Bill makes a journal entry. "One half hour discussing settlement posture with counsel for Neverpay, Inc." He drums his fingers. Maybe he should see what counsel for the other co-defendant is thinking too . . . .

Lawyers have four traditional methods of charging clients:

1. <u>Hourly rates</u>. Here, the firm charges a certain amount for every fraction of an hour that any "timekeeper" (lawyer or paralegal) at the firm devotes to the matter.

2. <u>Lump sums</u>. The lump sum arrangement sets a specific cost for the handling of a certain matter, regardless of the work actually done.

3. <u>Contingency fees</u>. The contingency fee gives the lawyer a share of the proceeds collected from the litigation. Most commonly used by lawyers representing plaintiffs in personal injury cases, the contingency fee is now becoming more common in commercial cases.

4. <u>Retainers.</u> Less common than it used to be, the retainer is an arrangement whereby a client pays a lump sum to a firm to handle all or a designated portion of the client's legal problems over a specific period. (Aside from designating a fee structure, the word "retainer" is also commonly used to refer to a deposit against hourly fees).

This chapter addresses hourly rates. It also reviews the use of lump sums in litigation. The following chapter, *Booty and Bounties*, discusses contingency fees and combination arrangements.

1. __The Hourly Rate Method__

Hourly rates are one of the common punching bags when people speak of "cleaning up" the legal system. The impression seems to be that a lawyer once thought up the hourly rate as a new way to gouge a client. The truth is, it used to be very common for a lawyer and a client to agree to a lump sum based on the value of the lawyer's work to the client. Many clients grew to see the hourly method as a more scientific way to measure value.

There is no method that cannot be abused. Understand the reasons for each method, and its components and variations. Only then can you choose the method that is best for you.

The key terms of an hourly rate arrangement are:

o   the amount per hour each professional will charge;

o   the minimum incremental units in which the charges will be calculated; and

o   the types and amounts of costs which will be charged in addition to professional services.

__Amount Per Hour__

Amounts per hour range widely according to geographic area, seniority, and area of specialization.

Senior partner vs. associate.

Generally speaking, a fifty-year-old partner charges an hourly rate at least twice as high as a new associate. However, many sophisticated clients believe that they maximize the value of their legal dollar by using more senior attorneys. They believe that the inefficiencies caused by a young associate's inexperience are not always fully compensated by the savings in hourly rates.

Some law firms do tend to train associates at a client's expense. For legal research and for drafting simple documents, new associates may be very cost-effective. For other tasks, unless an associate has significant work experience prior to law school, or has served as a law clerk for a trial judge, he begins a career with a need for substantial on-the-job training. Partners are sometimes reluctant to reduce or "write down" the billable hours over-expended by a green associate. They rationalize that any inefficiencies are offset by the associate's lower rates. In some cases this is true, but certainly not in all.

Don't panic.

It would be wrong to react with an overly dim view of the use of associates. A senior associate (one who has been at the firm several years, but has not yet been accepted into partnership) often combines the best of all variables: the substantial experience and maturity of a young partner, combined with a comparatively low rate and a continuing desire to prove oneself. Even very young associates can do certain things more cost-effectively than their superiors.

The key is for a senior attorney to manage junior partners and associates so that each lawyer works on separate parts of a project, chosen to balance cost against necessary expertise. A lawyer with a sensitivity to the problem and to the client's interests can use associates very effectively. The point is simply that this needs monitoring.

Minimum Increments

Another variable is the minimum unit for recording time. Most law firms bill in minimum increments of 1/10 to 1/4 of an hour. The difference can be significant. Assume a client calls and the lawyer speaks with him for five minutes, and that no preparation or follow-up by the lawyer is required. The lawyer has just performed legal services for 1/12 of an hour. If the lawyer bills in units of 1/10, he will bill the telephone call as 1/10 of an hour. If the lawyer's hourly rate is $100, the client will be charged $10.00. However, if the lawyer's firm uses the minimum increment of 1/4, then the client will be charged for 1/4 of an hour's worth of service, or $25.00 for the same telephone call.

For more highly paid lawyers, minimum increments make a bigger difference. If the lawyer bills at the rate of $400.00 per hour, then, under the same facts, the client will pay $100 for the phone call when the firm bills on quarter-hour increments. If the firm bills in hourly increments of one-tenth, the client would pay only $40.00.

Aggregating minimum increments can affect your bill.

Suppose the same lawyer engages in not one five-minute conversation with a client, but two five-minute conversations five hours apart. Does the quarter-hour biller charge two quarter hours (thirty minutes) for ten minutes of his time?

These problems are minor when the legal work involves large chunks of continuous time. However, various matters require frequent but short communications. The more frequent and short these are, the more the client pays a premium for the lawyer's time. Furthermore, it is often the lawyer with the highest billing rate who is engaged during the shortest increments of time. Therefore, the premiums resulting from the increment system are often being charged against the highest rates.

Good lawyers make sure minimum increments do not penalize you.

To compensate, many partners or supervising lawyers do some oversight at no charge. These supervising lawyers see their role in part as traffic directors, and realize that the billings compiled by the junior attorneys whom they supervise amply justify the partner's uncharged time.

Other partners who do record and bill for this time see to it that the increment system does not gouge the client. Where items of time are recorded periodically over a day, many lawyers make sure that the increment does not exaggerate time more than once. Many record time only when it reaches a threshold close to the minimum increment.

The point again is not to have an automatic reaction, but to look for the *value* you are getting. In some cases, the lawyer's few minutes of advice is more valuable than the several hours he may later spend in a deposition. Don't think of the increments system as a bugaboo, but as another billing component to understand. Make your comprehension of it a tool in evaluating the lawyer's bills.

Costs and Overhead

Simple enough so far, right? The lawyer can charge you the market rate for his time. And of course, it is only natural for the client to reimburse the firm for out-of-pocket advances made on the client's behalf. These expenses can include costs charged by courts for filing pleadings; by court reporters for transcribing depositions; and by mortgage offices for recording mortgages and judgments. It is fair for you to pay for air fare, hotel and meals incurred during out-of-town travel in your service.

Travel time.

What about paying the lawyer's hourly rate while he is reading a mystery novel on the plane? Travel time is not a unit of what the lawyer has to sell -- his expertise. A few of the largest clients, whose volume of work gives them some bargaining power, refuse to pay for it at all. On the other hand, if it were not for your case, the lawyer could be home playing with his children, or in his office earning fees from one of his other clients. Ask your lawyer at the outset how he handles travel time and whether he foresees any need for it in your case. If the travel will be substantial, perhaps you can negotiate a reduced rate for travel time, particularly travel that occurs outside ordinary working hours.

"Emergency" overhead.

Unless you get a sweetheart hourly rate, you should resist any attempt to bill you for routine overhead. That is a consideration in setting the hourly rates. You also have a right to question overtime and extra costs of meeting deadlines when a true emergency was not involved.

Overtime performed in extraordinary circumstances is a fair subject for negotiation. Consider an arrangement to *share* such costs. This gives the lawyer an incentive to keep them to a minimum.

Meals.

What about meals eaten by associates whom your case requires to stay at the office until late at night? If you pay for the time, the firm can pick up the cost of the meal.

A perspective.

The illustration of excessive out-of-pocket costs given at the beginning of Section Four does not represent a typical law firm. On the other hand, neither is it a bogeyman story. In fact, an article in the September 1991 issue of *The American Lawyer* reported respectable firms charging $33.60 for coffee, juice and Danish for four associates; $22.00 to carry a document ten blocks; $360 for letting a client use a conference room; $45.00 per hour for secretarial and word processing staff totalling $310,645 in one major case alone; and $42,386 for meals for lawyers and staff working on the same case. These examples were only a few of the charges reported in the article.

In the vast majority of bills, costs are a small item compared with the fees themselves. However, they can add up. Insist on a list of the costs the law firm expects to charge to you. Negotiate any that are unreasonable in light of all the circumstances. Refuse to pay for any *types* of costs you have not authorized.

2. Lump Sums

Chapter Six explains the use of lump sum fees in transaction work. A lump sum fee may also be useful in litigation for routine and repetitive items. For example, you may agree with your small collections lawyer to pay $30 for a demand letter and $200 to file a simple complaint, if necessary. After the debtor files his responsive pleading, you can decide whether further routine actions are called for, or whether the issues raised now call for non-routine work compensable at an hourly rate.

Engagement letters are fine, but not as a substitute for bargaining.

Many firms use *engagement letters* to define their relationship with their clients. An engagement letter is a good idea. If your lawyer does not offer you such a letter, consider asking for one. But don't let a standardized engagement letter substitute for the discussions with your lawyer that this Section recommends. Most form engagement letters are vague and one-sided. Make sure that the one you sign incorporates the terms you negotiate.

One firm or several?

Do you have more bargaining power on fees if you spread your work around to several firms? Some in-house counsel for large corporations think so. Others believe that using a single firm creates a mutual familiarity that is beneficial, as long as the firm has the expertise for the different kinds of work you require.

A lawyer died and ascended to Heaven. Awaiting admission, he said to Saint Peter, "Listen, I'm not usually a complainer, and I _am_ happy to be here. But I do feel that I was taken in my prime. You know, I was only forty-four years old."

Saint Peter's face clouded, and he opened a notebook. "There must be some mistake. According to your law firm's time sheets, you're a hundred and five."[1]

---

[1]Did you ever notice that so many of the most time-honored lawyer jokes involve lawyers in Heaven?

Chapter Thirteen

Booty and Bounties

Long ago, before great nation-states could afford standing armies, medieval kings recruited soldiers with the promise of captured treasure. The English yeomen at Agincourt spent as much time relieving the dead of their belongings as they did in killing them. Military historians rank booty and ransom high among the motivations that gave soldiers the will to combat.[2]

Hourly rates and lump sums are not lines in the sand that you cannot cross. Modern litigators will consider taking their pay from enemy casualties, too. Also, as the market for legal services becomes more competitive, more lawyers will discuss alternatives or combinations that allow them to make a living, but which also charge you according to value and in keeping with the economics of your case. This chapter discusses contingency fees and "incentive" or combination arrangements.

1. Economics of the Contingency Fee

Contingency fees are easiest to arrange when you are the plaintiff--that is, when you are the party who seeks to

---

[2]John Keegan, *The Face of Battle* (Viking Penguin, Inc., 1976).

recover money from the other side. Rather than bill you by the hour, the lawyer ties his fee to the amount you recover. Fees ranging from twenty-five to forty percent of the recovery are standard; one-third is the most common.

The chief advantage to you is that you have no risk of unrecovered fees. A contingency fee is especially attractive if your claim has a significant risk of defeat or of non-collection. When you use a contingency-fee contract, your only risk is your liability for "costs." More about that later.

Consider using the contingency fee to finance legal services.

The contingency fee grew out of personal-injury litigation, where having to pay an hourly rate would have denied many a longshoreman's widow her day in court. Now, contingency fees are becoming popular among business plaintiffs. For example, a bank that has written off a loan may have some chance of collecting, but it would be reluctant to risk sending more good money after bad. A number of firms specializing in collections will take such cases on a contingency fee. Even the most conservative lawyers, jealous of law school classmates getting rich overnight in the plaintiffs' bar, are handling more "garden variety" commercial claims on contingency fees.

Beware of counterclaims.

Contingency fees are best suited for cases where the only real issues are the yes-or-no question of your opponent's liability and the amount of damages. A contingency fee is risk-free only if there are no claims that the person you are suing might bring against you. Your contingency-fee lawyer will not share your exposure on a counterclaim. In fact, if the counterclaim raises significant new issues requiring his attention, the lawyer may have to add an hourly arrangement for that part of his work that is peculiar to defending the counterclaim. Make sure you evaluate the risk of a counterclaim before you decide whether to sue, and what fee arrangement to use.

Costs Again

You can expect your contingency-fee lawyer to cover routine costs out of his percentage share of the contingency award. These will include his secretary and office staff, office rent and equipment. Usually, however, your lawyer will also incur expenses specific to your case: filing fees for pleadings, expert witness fees, court reporter fees for deposition transcripts, and travel costs. These costs are usually deducted from the recovery *before* your lawyer's percentage fee is calculated.

Risk of non-recovery.

In personal-injury cases, the contingency-fee lawyer ordinarily bears the risk of unrecovered costs. That is not necessarily true for business clients. Make sure you understand who will be responsible for costs. If he will not be responsible, then ask him to estimate costs for you. You can then take them into account in deciding whether to sue.

Use Fee Discussions for Case Analysis

Your lawyer is not required to accept a contingency arrangement. However, he should not charge you for the time he spends in negotiating the fee. His decision whether to accept your case on contingency gives you some free and meaningful feedback on the merits and economics of your claim. If a lawyer declines to take your claim except on an hourly basis, that is a signal that the economics of suing may be poor.

Example 1.

If your lawyer declines to accept a $10,000 claim on a thirty percent contingency, that could mean several things. Maybe he would expect to incur substantially more than $3000 worth of his time. Maybe he sees a substantial risk of defeat. Maybe he doubts that the judgment would be collectible. If raising the percentage does not cure the problem, this means his analysis of the economics of your case is even more pessimistic.

If your lawyer will not take your claim on a contingency fee, ask him to specify his concerns. This knowledge will help you decide whether to go forward even on an hourly basis.

Example 2.

Under the same facts, assume that the lawyer declines a fifty percent contingency fee because he thinks he would incur about fifty hours of his time, which he values at $100 per hour, and sees only a forty-percent chance of collection, based on the debtor's financial condition. If the lawyer offers to accept the case on an hourly basis at $100 per hour, your answer should be "No." You would expect to pay him $5000 for an average projected recovery of $4000 ($10,000 claim, multiplied by a forty percent chance of collection). Your only economical choice, assuming that his analysis is well-considered, is to look for another lawyer -- even a less talented one -- who will accept the case on a contingency fee or at a lower hourly rate.

A larger amount in dispute will improve the economics.

The size of the claim dramatically affects the economics of the case and of the fee arrangement. Generally speaking, the larger the amount in dispute, the more time the lawyer will spend in its prosecution or defense. However, the attorneys fees do not increase at the same pace as the size of the claim. Thus, if someone owes you $300,000, a forty-percent risk of non-collection might not deter the same contingency fee lawyer who declined to accept your $10,000 claim.

As the economics of your case improve (that is, as the amount at stake increases, as the chances of success brighten, or as the collection risk diminishes), the percentage paid to your lawyer should go down. For a small case or one of doubtful collectibility, a fifty percent contingency fee may be reasonable and the best you can get. A contingency percentage can go as low as ten percent in a big case with a high probability of success. There is no reason in the world not to seek bids from several lawyers, as long as you are comfortable with each one's skill.

Shifting Percentages

You can agree that the contingency percentage will change according to several variables within a case.

Incentives of the contingency fee.

A litigator working for an hourly fee has every incentive to prepare the case as thoroughly as possible. This is precisely what you would want, if only each unit of work did not cost you an extra unit of fees. As your hourly litigator maximizes your chances of success, your "victory" may prove to cost more than a loss.

With a contingency fee, on the other hand, the litigator -- not you -- bears the risk of overpreparing. More times than not, this is to your advantage. If your case were the only one the lawyer was handling, your respective interests would be very similar. When the litigator has several cases pending, however, his interests may be different from yours.

Assume that your lawyer is handling ten claims of $100,000 each, including yours. Assume that with a certain amount of work -- say fifty hours -- your chances of winning would be fifty percent. Assume that spending twenty-five more hours would increase your chances of winning to sixty percent. If the lawyer has only 500 hours to spend on all ten of his cases, he is better off dividing his time equally.

You would be better off if he spent the extra twenty-five hours on your case.

This is a good example of a case that might call for shifting percentages.

The percentage can increase with stages of litigation.

For example, the lawyer and his client may agree that if the lawyer can settle the case before trial, his share will be twenty-five percent or thirty percent. They may also agree that if he is required to take the case through trial (and possibly through appeal), then his share will be forty percent or fifty percent. This arrangement, however roughly, at least creates some relationship between work required and compensation. At the same time, it may create disincentives for the lawyer to push for settlement at or near those junctures that result in a percentage increase.

The percentage can increase with the amount recovered.

You may also agree with your lawyer to give him one third of all amounts recovered up to a certain number, and one-half of any amounts beyond that. This sort of arrangement can be very meaningful if the case presents a range of possible damage amounts due to possible findings of comparative negligence, or complexity in the damage claims. It encourages your lawyer to invest extra time if doing so will benefit you both.

The variations outlined above (increasing the percentage based on the progress of the litigation or on the amount recovered) enable you to negotiate an arrangement to make sure that the lawyer's incentives closely reflect your interests.

2. Combination Arrangements

Combination arrangements are another way lawyers and their clients can improve the economics of legal representation.

A lump sum, plus reduced hourly fee, can improve the economics of defending.

Assume you are defending a claim for $100,000. Your lawyer gives you a fifty percent chance of winning. At an hourly rate of $100, your lawyer estimates a cost of defense in the range of $30,000 to $60,000. Based on these estimates, defending is cost-effective if the lawyer spends less than 500 hours. If he spends more than 500 hours, then your cost (over $50,000) and your projected loss after litigating ($50,000) would exceed the claim.

You could improve the economics by a combination lump sum and hourly fee. For example, if you paid a lump sum of $35,000, plus $50 per hour after he has spent 350 hours, you benefit because your lawyer would have to spend 650 hours before defending became uneconomical. Your lawyer benefits because he still beats his minimum projection of $30,000, without committing to a ceiling.

A lump sum, plus a reduced contingency percentage, can improve the economics of prosecuting.

Assume that your claim to recover $100,000 receives a cold response from the lawyers you have consulted. Justice is on your side, they say, but the law probably is not; estimates range from a ten percent to thirty percent likelihood of success. No one is excited about taking it on a contingency. You wish to pursue the case for reasons of principle, but not if it will cost you more than $50,000 to pursue. Why not offer the lawyer a $20,000 lump sum against a thirty percent contingency fee? Alternatively, you can offer to pay a regular or reduced hourly rate up to $20,000 with a thirty percent contingency fee *on top* of the lump sum figure.

Reward a litigator for coming in under budget.

A different approach might be, after you have received the case plan and budget from your lawyer, to agree to pay him a certain percentage of any amount by which he comes in below the estimate.

Raise your consciousness.

These sorts of hybrid arrangements should be considered whenever the expected range of fees on an hourly basis straddles the threshold between an economical and an uneconomical prosecution or defense. The foregoing examples are oversimplified for the sake of illustration. Actual calculations, of course, should consider the time value of money, legal interest, costs, and possible recovery of attorneys fees.

The possible combinations are limited only by the circumstances of the case, by your understanding of the basic fee structures and how they work, and by the creativity of you and your lawyer. The point is, a number of goals which may not be economical under any of the traditional fee situations may well become mutually desirable under some more creative structure.

The American Bar Association has published a book, *Beyond the Billable Hour* (1989), that explains value billing, flat rates, cost-plus billing, and incentive billing. Although it is addressed to lawyers rather than clients, you may find it very informative. At a cost of $79.95, however, you may be tempted to borrow it from a lawyer or read it in a law library.

Proposing a creative arrangement is not radical or rude.

Creative fee arrangements can be had not only with small or unknown firms, but with prestigious firms as well. According to a February 3, 1992, article in *Of Counsel*, Houston's forty-one-lawyer firm of Susman Godfrey recruits from the top echelons of the nation's best law schools. Its revenues and profits are enviable.

According to the article, Susman Godfrey actually encourages clients to suggest creative billing proposals, which reward the firm for achieving desired results in litigation. In one case, for example, senior partner Steve

117

Susman gave a thirty percent discount in his hourly rate, but the client agreed to pay a $2,000,000 bonus if Susman obtained a desired result. In another case, Susman agreed to make his rate depend on the result obtained.

Many lawyers would have resisted such an arrangement ten years ago. In today's market, however, it is by no means unthinkable. If your litigator is unreceptive to discussing alternatives on their merits, do not let him convince you that you are being unrealistic in asking to discuss them.

Your relationship with your lawyer is a business relationship. Give it the same consideration you give your other vendor relationships. If your lawyer is open-minded, you can both benefit.

Chapter Fourteen

Plan of Battle

Jeff is highly motivated. As a new associate, Jeff understands that his evaluations and bonus will depend largely on his billable hours. Lately, he has been short on assignments. Now he is sitting in the office of Perry, the senior partner. Perry explains that the client is defending a claim for defects and breach of warranty. The client is headquartered here in Pacific Rim, California. The purchaser is headquartered in Boston. The sale agreement does not contain a choice of law provision. It is unclear whether Massachusetts or California law should apply. This needs research.

"We've got to be right on this," says Perry. "If there's a hole in our research, we can be assured that opposing counsel will embarrass us. I want your research to be conclusive and exhaustive."

Jeff nods earnestly. In his own mind, however, he is already calculating the potential. "This deserves fifty hours at least," he thinks to himself. Jeff trudges off contentedly to the library.

Before your lawyer does any work, you need a case plan and budget. The case plan provides the best opportunity to make sure you and your lawyer truly understand each other about the cost of going forward. It enables you to evaluate your lawyer's economic management of your case. It gives you a background against which to process new information, and to recognize any changes in the economics of settlement.

This chapter tells you what a case plan should contain. It explains how to use a case plan. It even suggests how to ask for one.

1. What A Case Plan Should Contain.

A case plan and budget for a plaintiff might contain the following components:

1. Actions required to bring the case to conclusion;

2. Cost (or range of costs) of each action so listed;

3. Probable time frame for completion;

4. Percentage likelihood of possible outcomes; and

5. Prospects of collection.

Sample Case Plan

The credit buyer of your software system owes you $80,000. After the buyer fails to return your telephone calls and ignores your demand letters, you engage counsel to reduce the claim to judgment. The lawyer provides you the following case plan:

1. *Actions required:*

   a. *Preparation and filing of complaint - $600.*

   b. *Preparation of requests for admission and interrogatories - $700.*

   c. *(If responses to requests for admission are favorable and raise no material fact issues) Motion for Summary Judgment: preparation - $3,000; argument - $500.*

   d. *(If Answer or discovery responses raise questions of fact) Taking and defending approximately 4 depositions, including preparation and costs of transcription - $3,500.*

   e. *(If responses to discovery do not support motion for summary judgment) Preparation for and conducting trial, including preparation of witnesses, drafting of trial memorandum, organization of exhibits - $7,000.*

   f. *Costs of executing judgment - $2,000.*

   Summary: If discovery responses raise no important fact issues, the budget will include items a, b, c and f. Total cost - $6,800.

   If there are material fact issues, the budget will include items a, b, d, e and f. Total cost - $13,800.

Both scenarios assume no appeal. If necessary to prosecute or defend appeal, add $8,000.

2. *Time frame: If no fact issues are raised by pleadings or written discovery and motion for summary judgment is available, approximately 3 to 9 months. Otherwise, if trial is required, between 9 months and 2 years, depending on availability of trial dates on court docket.*

3. *Likelihood of success. Customer complaints mentioned in interview would not ordinarily excuse payment under the sale agreement. Unless pleadings and discovery reveal new fact issues not previously discussed, chances of obtaining favorable judgment are eighty percent.*

4. *Risk of collection. Dun and Bradstreet listing reveals no credit problems. Search of court records reveals no judgments recorded against defendant. Because defendant is not publicly traded, detailed financial information is not publicly available. NEXIS research reveals no adverse news articles. Client did not obtain financial statements during negotiations. Therefore, the only basis for doubting ability to pay judgment is the customer's failure to pay to date. Subject to further information suggested by discovery, estimated probability of collection is eighty percent.*

2. Using the Case Plan.

Your case plan confirms whether you understand the lawyer.

In the example, the case plan indicates that you will spend at least $6,800 to collect. The case plan further indicates that you may spend $13,800, and, if the trial judgment is appealed, that you would spend $21,800.

The range of expenses must be compared to your expected real recovery. According to the case plan, if you win, you will receive a judgment for $80,000. Multiply $80,000 times the estimated eighty percent probability of success, and you have a projected case value of $64,000. Discount that figure by the risk of non-collection ($64,000 multiplied by an eighty percent chance of collection). This leaves you with a legitimate expectation of $51,200. This expectation exceeds even the highest estimates of going forward. Based on those numbers, and assuming that settlement cannot be negotiated, the economics are in favor of proceeding.

What your case plan cannot do.

If you think of your case plan and budget as a stone tablet, you will probably be disappointed. If you are looking for economic certainty, ask for a lump sum agreement. A case plan and budget have a different purpose. They offer a way to improve your communication with your lawyer. Not every deviation from the plan is your lawyer's fault.

Remember, one of the biggest problems with litigation is that so much depends on the actions of the opponent.

Think of your case plan as a fluid document.

Revise the plan as the case evolves. Every bill should contain a summary of total charges from the date your lawyer opened the file (See Chapter Fifteen). You can measure this summary against the case plan. Every quarter or so, you should review the case plan with your lawyer and determine whether any revisions are in order.

o   Has the other side defended more tenaciously than expected? Does this mean more discovery will be required? If so, how much more will it cost?

o   Has the defendant said anything that changes the percentage likelihood of a favorable judgment? What is the new percentage?

o   Does the lawyer have any more insight into the defendant's financial condition?

Suppose your lawyer tells you that the defendant has transferred all its assets to defeat your attempts at collection. Reaching those assets will certainly raise new issues and probably make summary judgment impossible.

Your lawyer believes that it will also make the trial likely to cost at least $20,000 if there is no appeal. Assume further that new allegations of defects have arisen in discovery. Your lawyer now advises that these fact issues reduce your chances of recovery to one-half. Now an investment of at least $20,000 would be required to obtain a fifty percent likelihood of an $80,000 judgment. This gives you a probable judgment value of $40,000. Discount the resulting $40,000 by the new probability of collection (now only sixty percent) to $24,000. Under these facts, if you can settle for $30,000, that would now appear to be a good outcome. Under the original plan, it would not.

Use your case plan to evaluate your lawyer's economic performance.

If the plan calls for total fees of $20,000, and you have paid that much after only four months, ask for an explanation. If a change in circumstances does not fully explain the difference, a "write-down" or reduction of your bill might be in order.

Even if you never actually ask for a write-down, this process effectively keeps your lawyer's eye on the economic ball. The best lawyers are stingy with their time anyway, knowing that it is costing you money. Many, however, benefit from gentle reminders. The lawyer who is conscious of being watched is less likely to dream up extensive research ideas. He is also less likely to fire off second rounds of written discovery, without first explaining the potential benefits to you and getting you to "buy in" to this new investment of his time.

3. <u>How to Ask for a Case Plan</u>.

Dear Perry:

I am excited at the prospect of using your services. You come highly recommended by our accountants, who have worked with you successfully in a variety of situations.

Before we initiate any work, I would like to meet with you to review a case plan and budget. My experience has been that doing one of these up front clarifies my expectations and almost always makes for a better relationship.

Please give some thought to the likely stages of this litigation and to the probabilities and ranges of costs for each. I would expect an initial pleadings stage, preliminary motions, discovery, pretrial motions, trial and appeal. If there will be others, let me know.

I realize that Suitprone's activities will determine a great deal of the costs. That is why I think ranges are better than absolute numbers. But in giving me the range of costs, I hope you will also be able to give me some idea of how firm you think they are.

I suggest you prepare these informally for our initial meeting, where we can discuss them and then put them in writing for my benefit in monitoring the case. Please bill me for your time in preparing the plan, but please devote no more than thirty minutes to working on this before we meet.

Again, I anticipate a relationship that benefits us both, and I certainly look forward to meeting you.

Sincerely,

John Doe

Some lawyers who are unused to case plans and budgets resist them. However, more and more institutional clients have come to insist on them as a matter of course.

Now, in fact, many lawyers actually like using a case plan. It enables the litigator to verify that he and his client are "on the same page." The case plan can protect the lawyer from unwarranted complaints about his bills. Asking for a case plan is simply an example of the client and the lawyer *doing the thing right.*

If your lawyer resists giving a case plan, he probably has no experience with it. Reassure him that it can benefit him as well as you. Tell him you will compensate him for preparing it at his usual hourly rate (although one hour should usually be enough). Remind him that the plan will not create a lump sum contract. You should, however, reserve the right to object to unexplained deviations. If all your reassurances do not convince him, then only the highest confidence in his skills would justify using him.

Chapter Fifteen

Feeding the Bulldog

Mr. John Doe
101 New Age Boulevard
Pacific Rim, CA

Dear John:

I am pleased to enclose the settlement check received from Suitprone Enterprises for $200,000. Also enclosed please find our statement for services performed in the subject litigation, in the total amount of $150,000. Although this is somewhat higher than we originally estimated, the work proved to be more substantial than we could have foreseen.

Note that the settlement check is made payable to your company and to its attorneys. Please endorse the check and return it to me. We will add our own endorsement, run it through our trust account, and forward your $50,000 share.

With best regards, I remain

Sincerely,

Perry

This kind of surprise bill can be prevented by interim bills or at least statements of account status. This chapter will explain what bills should contain, when to receive them, and how to use them to monitor your case.

1. <u>What a Bill Should Tell You</u>.

All bills should contain the following:

a. a description of the services performed and of the costs incurred;

b. the identity and role of the people who performed the services;

c. the date the services were performed;

d. the amount of time spent in performing them; and

e. the hourly rate charged by each "timekeeper."

This is a simplified version of an acceptable bill:

Date	Activity	Timekeeper	Hours	Rate	Total
4/1/92	Initial meeting with client, reviewed files, meeting with associate to give instructions on preparation of initial responsive pleadings.	John Doe	2.5	$200.00	$500.00
4/1/92	Meeting John Doe to receive instructions on preparation of pleadings, reviewed file, drafted initial responsive pleadings.	Jane Roe	3.5	$90.00	$315.00
	Total for April, 1992				$815.00

You should not accept a mere summary.

Billing Statement for Time Period Beginning
August 1, 1992, through August 30, 1992

Various conferences with client
and between responsible attorneys;
review of file, drafting of initial
responsive pleadings. $815.00

Work-unit bills.

Many institutional users of lawyers go one step further. On top of a summary of the work a particular lawyer performed on a given day and the time devoted to it, they require the lawyer to break down the time spent on each specific service.

Date	Activity	Timekeeper	Hours	Rate	Total
4/1/92	Initial meeting with client (1.0); reviewed files (1.0); meeting with associate to give instructions on preparations of initial responsive pleadings (.5)	John Doe	2.5	$200.00	$500.00
4/1/92	Meeting with John Doe to receive instructions on preparation of pleadings (.5); reviewed file (1.0); drafted initial responsive pleadings (2.0)	Jane Roe	3.5	$90.00	$315.00
	Total for April, 1992				$815.00

This method improves your ability to review the management of your case. It may also increase your lawyer's consciousness of the fact that you are watching his case management.

Ask for a summary or running total.

Another part of your bill should be the summary of fees and costs incurred to date. This running total is as meaningful as the current bill itself. Certainly you could obtain a summary yourself simply by adding your previous bills to the total. However, most firms with modern equipment can make this a part of your bill with little extra effort. It is also good for the lawyer reviewing your bills to see the running total with each billing. NOTE: *Make sure you add to your running total any expenses that you have paid directly, such as local counsel or expert witness fees.*

2. __Timing of the Bill__

The firm reduces its collection spread by billing you monthly. Considering the time value of money and for simplicity of accounting, you might prefer to pay quarterly or even on completion. However, unless you have special bargaining power, you will probably have some difficulty talking a firm out of a monthly billing arrangement.

One advantage of monthly billing is that it helps you spot problems before they have gotten out of hand. Some clients insist on monthly billings for this reason. Even if you negotiate a longer term billing system for financial reasons, you would still be wise to ask for a monthly statement.

3. __How to Use a Bill.__

The properly done bill enables you to see how much you invested in each item of work. Use your bill to compare results against your case plan estimates. Use it to identify work outside the case plan, and to find waste. You need not be an expert to find inefficiencies in a bill. The simplest things to identify also happen to be the biggest problem areas:

1. Overstaffing - Is there a good reason to have two attorneys at a deposition?

2. <u>Excessive discovery</u> - Litigators are afraid of leaving any helpful evidence undiscovered. At some point, the law of diminishing returns applies.

3. <u>Excessive research</u> - This is where a bill can get out of control. Consider asking for prior approval rights. Ask the attorney to justify research, especially if the research is in an area of his particular expertise.

4. <u>Turnover</u> - Is your file a revolving door of associates? Are the replacements "getting up to speed" at your expense?

Compare the bill to the case plan and budget.

You should explain in advance that you will not approve any bill for payment that puts the file total over budget, unless your lawyer has already talked to you and you have agreed to a new budget before the bill is sent.

Compare the bill to your own notes.

Some business managers who oversee litigation keep logs and calendars on each case. They enter dates, times, and lengths of all meetings and telephone conferences with their lawyers. They compare their notes to bills to check for discrepancies.

How to address bill problems.

In many large cities there are "legal audit" firms of lawyers and accountants who will review bills. Unless you have massive bills, however, hiring a legal audit firm may cost more than it saves. If you believe that the bills are inflated or show real inefficiencies, call your lawyer. He may be more easily convinced to reduce it than you expect. Most studies and audits of billings indicate that excesses are not usually the result of fraud but, far more often, of carelessness and inefficiency. If you really believe your law firm is flim-flamming you, you are using the wrong firm.

Chapter Sixteen

News From the Front

You are sitting at the counsel's table. Your lawyer's chair beside you is empty. She is standing. All eyes are on her as she cross-examines the defendant. The witness knows he is in trouble. He is getting angry. He tries to argue with your lawyer. Your lawyer turns a verbal pirouette, like a matador with an angry bull. Now the defendant is red in the face.

You have never seen your lawyer like this. At first, you were not entirely sure that this prim intellectual was such a good recommendation. Now you are a believer. She finishes with a series of hammer-blow leading questions. No one on the jury doubts any longer that the defendant infringed your patent. You can almost see blindfolded Justice lifting her scales.

Finally, it is your turn to take the stand again. Just a few more questions from the defendant's lawyer. Responding, you agree with one of his characterizations. "Yes, I guess you could say my invention was obvious. But I was the first one with the tenacity to create it."

You look at your lawyer to see how you are doing. She is staring at you. Her mouth hangs open. You notice that now she is the one who is red. You begin to wonder if maybe you should have told her this earlier.

How much should you involve yourself in the litigation? The answer has two simple but important components:

1. Your lawyer's need for information from you; and

2. Your need for information from the lawyer.

1. Satisfying Your Lawyer's Need for Information from You

Your lawyer can only represent you well if he is fully informed of all the material facts pertaining to your case. He must also understand your operations and your industry in general.

Nothing will frustrate your lawyer more than to learn important facts late in the case that you should have communicated long before. This is especially true when the facts surface without warning and at a critical time such as at a trial or hearing. You may feel that frustrating lawyers is a good thing. However, your case will suffer as well.

Concerns about sharing information with your lawyer are generally misplaced.

Clients withhold information from their lawyers for a number of reasons. Some are propelled by vanity. Others may be afraid of losing the lawyer, or have some notion that a lawyer can best represent them only if ignorant of their faults. These feelings are misguided. Would you conceal your medical history from your doctor?

A good litigator does not represent someone less zealously after learning his failings. Indeed, the opposite may often be true. When a lawyer thinks the client is clearly right, he sometimes lapses into a certain feeling of self-righteousness. In so doing, the litigator risks losing touch with the horrifying fear of defeat, a fear which, when properly channeled, is the wellspring of inspired advocacy.

Psychology aside, knowing your weak points will be of vital necessity, both in advising you of your options, and in preparing for battle. Your litigator continually searches for ways to avoid or neutralize your points of vulnerability. This can only occur if he knows what they are.

A lawyer is forbidden by law to reveal what you tell him in confidence, except in limited circumstances, such as to prevent a crime that is planned or in process.

Make sure you understand what information your lawyer needs.

Clients sometimes fail to give information because they simply do not know its importance. It is the lawyer's responsibility to ask for the most critical information at the outset. However, it is impossible for him to cover every conceivable base. Try to understand the dispute and offer any facts that might be pertinent.

Make sure that the lawyer understands your operations. List everyone who has information about the case. Give the nature and location of documents and any known statements (written or unwritten) made by your opponent. Volunteer

137

evidence of any kind that tends to support *or contradict* your version of the facts.

Communicate early.

One of the earliest things that should happen when you retain counsel is a face-to-face meeting where the fullest possible exchange occurs. The lawyer will represent you best *and most cheaply* if he receives the maximum information from the outset.

2. Receiving Information from Your Lawyer

You will be called upon to make important decisions during the litigation, particularly whether to settle. It is therefore critical that you have information germane to the decision.

Start from the beginning and update.

At the beginning, ask your lawyer to identify and prioritize the issues of fact and law that will control the outcome of the case. Ask him to assign probabilities to each variable that affects the expected outcome. Ask for the probable *quantum*, or dollar recovery, attributable to the various outcomes. Against these possibilities, balance your lawyer's estimate of the costs of going forward, and the amounts for which he believes the case could be settled.

Updating this information will keep you in a position to make informed decisions. If several months have passed with no significant discussions, review with your lawyer the most recent set of information and estimates he has provided. Ask whether he would revise anything in light of more recent developments. Do the same after an important deposition, a pretrial conference, or meeting with the judge. Always update your information when you are evaluating a settlement offer.

Benefit from court appearances and conferences with the judge.

Unless the cost would be unusual, or the case is very small, consider attending non-routine court appearances. The benefits are several. First, you can see your lawyer in action and thus can form first-hand impressions as to his ability. You can also observe the judge and learn something of his attitudes and qualifications. The judge's comments may even give you some feeling of his predisposition toward your case. These are much better seen first-hand than reported second-hand.

Of all the pretrial events you can attend, the most useful is a settlement conference with the judge. Most judges will make themselves available for this purpose. The conference can be structured so that the judge excuses either party at some point and speaks to each privately. In this way, each side's position can be discussed with some frankness. The judge's settlement recommendations can provide great insight to a client who is otherwise reluctant to settle. If the lessons learned are painful, it is better to learn them before incurring the expense of a trial, and while some chance to negotiate remains. If such a conference is

139

scheduled, make every effort to attend. If one is not scheduled, consider asking the lawyer to try to arrange one.

Keep up with the paper flow.

You are entitled to receive copies of all pleadings, correspondence, discovery, and evidence received or produced by your lawyer. Receiving these documents will give you some basis to confirm or to interpret the summaries your lawyer provides. Even if you do not wish to read it all, you may still wish to receive it, for purposes of record-keeping or occasional spot-checking.

When you receive correspondence, read between the lines. Are your lawyer and the opposing counsel engaged in unnecessary quarrels? Do the activities that they are discussing correspond to your case plan and budget?

Again, even if you do not feel competent to second-guess your lawyer, or do not wish to devote the time to do so, asking for complete information at least gives your lawyer the sense that he is being monitored. Make sure, however, that this real or pretended monitoring does not dramatically increase your fees. Ask him to send the correspondence without explanatory cover letters, unless to call your attention to a truly critical development.

Respond to developing evidence.

Another reason for you to make sure you are receiving adequate information is to assure that you are sending enough information in the opposite direction, that is, back to your lawyer.

Deposition attendance provides a useful illustration of how to gauge your need for information. Here, at least four alternatives exist:

1. You can physically attend the deposition;

2. You can receive a complete transcript of the deposition;

3. You can ask for an outline of the deposition; or

4. You can get a one-page synopsis.

Example

You are negotiating with a software supplier to buy a new system for your public-relations firm. The system is not delivered and functioning until two months after the contract deadline. You lose ten customers. All of them mention that their decision was affected by the fact that you did not have the software system in place. The supplier does not respond to your demand letter, and you sue for your lost profits. The supplier's pleadings deny that time was of the essence. He alleges that during negotiations, several discussions were had concerning the impossibility of guaranteeing a delivery date. He claims that the contract deadline was intended only as a target date. The seller also pleads that your claims of lost profits are speculative.

Attend depositions if your presence is indispensable.

Using the example, when your lawyer takes the deposition of the supplier's representative who was present at the original negotiations, your physical presence might be useful. You are not allowed to rebut incorrect statements during the deposition. However, some of the seller's testimony will probably suggest follow-up questions which only you would know due to your participation in the negotiations. If you cannot attend, brief your lawyer thoroughly beforehand and read the complete deposition after it is transcribed.

Read the deposition transcript when your attendance is not practical.

Read the complete deposition when your physical presence is desirable but is not economical. Look for any misleading or inaccurate testimony. Explain to your lawyer precisely why it is false. Point him to any other evidence that will help him to correct or rebut it.

Ask for an outline if you have only partial knowledge of the subject matter.

Your lawyer or a paralegal can prepare an outline of the deponent's most important statements and annotate them by page number and line. In the example, assume that your lawyer deposes the seller's expert witness on damages. This deposition will reveal assumptions that the expert is making about your operations when he challenges your claims of lost profits. He may misunderstand your direct expense, your overhead, or your replacement capacity.

The outline will tell you where these sorts of information appear, and guide you to relevant source pages. Without reading the entire transcript, you can advise your lawyer of any errors in the facts that form the basis of the expert's opinion. *NOTE: The time spent in preparing such an outline is billed to you at an hourly rate, usually a paralegal's.*

In all other cases, ask for a one-page summary.

Experienced users of legal services often request a one-page summary of each deposition. A one-page summary demands very little of the preparer's billable time. Such a synopsis can be perfectly fine for a deposition of a friendly witness. Also, ask for one-page summaries whenever your personal knowledge does not enable you to challenge the witness' testimony. For example, a synopsis is probably all you need for an expert whose factual assumptions or opinions are beyond your ability to challenge.

Although it will probably not make the evening news, this subject is controversial. Some in-house claims managers insist on reading, or at least receiving, *all* depositions. They believe that the lawyer will never be certain what information the client has the ability to challenge. These suggestions are not offered as rules. Consider them tools as you apply the art of "clienting" to litigation.

Don't just call your lawyer and close your eyes.

If litigation is a battle, then your lawyer is clearly the general. It is usually a mistake to tell the general how to do the details of his job. You, however, are the commander-in-chief. You make the "big-picture" decisions about whether the war will be fought and how vigorously. Communication with your general -- in both directions -- is vital.

Chapter Seventeen

Debriefing

The jury filters back into the courtroom. All eyes are on the foreman as the judge asks for the verdict. "We, the jury, find that the defendant did <u>not</u> breach its warranty given to Suitprone Enterprises, Inc." You clasp your lawyer's hand. You glance at the lawyer for Suitprone, who was so condescending at your deposition. He doesn't look so condescending now.

At the victory dinner, your lawyer sips his single malt scotch. He contemplates this latest confirmation of his own sly indomitability, and savors the mild pulses of adrenalin as they slowly subside. You share his exultation. Your products have been fully vindicated. You congratulate yourself on your choice of a litigator. His performance in court has saved your company $200,000. You can put this one in the victory column and move forward.

Wait a minute. Because of the legal fees and costs you have incurred, you are $50,000 poorer than when suit began. Certainly, your victory was better than the alternative, but how would you like to do the whole thing over again a year later? The end of a trial (or consummation of a settlement) is the best time to consider preventive medicine for the future.

This kind of thinking comes more easily when you have lost. When you lose, it is natural, after criticizing the opponents' deceitfulness and the judge's bias, to consider the facts that seemed the most critical to your defeat.

You have the same opportunity to learn from a victory. After a few days (when he has finished reliving the highlights of the trial), ask your lawyer what advice he could give you to avoid similar disputes in the future. Unless you have a very close relationship with your lawyer, he may be reluctant to volunteer this sort of advice for fear of offending you. Encourage him to be candid.

Did you do the right thing?

Was the case a close call? If so, why? What were the positive facts that seemed most to influence the outcome in your favor? How can you reinforce those factors in the future?

Were you a jerk?

Did you miss any chances to prevent the dispute from ripening into litigation? Did you respond to Suitprone's demand letter with sarcasm, when a face-to-face meeting and a check for $5,000 could have settled everything? Is it possible that Suitprone's phone calls, which you failed to return, were simply honest efforts to find a way to reduce its damages?

Were you hanging around with a jerk?

Or was Suitprone, in hindsight, destined to litigate with you all along? Did you convince yourself that the strength of your product, or the force of your personality, would make you the first seller that had ever made Suitprone happy? Did you catch Suitprone making misleading statements, but shrug them off in the belief that your contract protected you?

Did you do the thing right?

Is it possible that Suitprone was sincere? However wrong Suitprone might have been, could Suitprone's reading of the contract have been as legitimate as yours? Could your agreement have been more clear about exactly what your product was supposed to do and what it could not? Would a written disclaimer, for example, have effectively disposed of the claims?

What did you learn about litigating?

Ask your lawyer how you did on the witness stand. How could you be a more convincing witness in the future? Ask him which of your employees seemed most credible on the stand. Which ones benefitted from pretrial discussions and which ones were "loose cannons"? Make some notes about which employees you would call as witnesses in the future.

Think of your litigation expenses as an investment in your own education.

Win, lose or settle, think of the money you pay to litigate not only as a cost of protecting your rights, but also as an educational investment. What did the case reveal about your compliance with the law? About your personality? About how you screen relationships? About the way you communicate and structure transactions? The money you have paid your litigator is only well spent if it buys you some knowledge as well.

So enjoy your victory dinner. After all you have been through, you certainly have it coming. But afterward, give some thought to how you can make another victory dinner unnecessary.

EPILOGUE

I cried when I wrote this song;
Sue me if I play too long.[3]

In protecting your business from litigation and legal costs, your shield, mace and body armor will be *communication*. Every problem addressed in this book directly reflects a failure to communicate.

Businesses that fail to *do the right thing* or that *hang around with jerks* have usually failed to take advantage of information that is available to them. Businesses that act like *jerks* and motivate someone to sue them seldom do so in dramatic ways. More often, they simply refuse to allow communication. When businesses neglect to *do the thing right*, they have failed to spend enough time and effort communicating.

The same is true of damage control. Effective settlement is nothing more than effective communication. The main reason arbitration is not more common is that too few clients -- and too few lawyers -- are familiar enough with it. If war indicates a failure of diplomacy, litigation shows a failure of communication.

Communication failures also account for the overly wide gulf between lawyers and clients. The problem would diminish if more lawyers knew how to think like clients. At

---

[3]Walter Becker and Donald Fagen, *Deacon Blues* (ABC Records, 1977).

the same time, clients would benefit by knowing more about how to think like lawyers.

Commit yourself to communicating better. It is difficult to succeed merely by knowing know more about your product than the next guy. If you run a business, you have to understand how to maneuver through our legal system. The secret is knowing how to *communicate* to avoid disputes, how to *communicate* to resolve disputes, and how to *communicate* to be an informed user of legal services.

This book is not the end of the discussion. It is barely a beginning. Every lawyer with any experience can offer entirely different and new suggestions. The point is that your business is not in a trackless jungle. There are some reliable paths you can follow. But it is up to you to choose them.

APPENDIX 1

Here is a list of American Arbitration offices, reprinted with permission of the American Arbitration Association:

<u>Northeast</u>

133 Federal Street
Boston, MA 02110-1703
(617) 451-6600/451-0763(Fax)

585 Stewart Ave., Suite 302
Garden City, NY 11530-4789
(516) 222-1660/745-6447(Fax)

Two Hartford Square West
Hartford, CT 06106-1943
(203) 278-5000/246-8442(Fax)

265 Davidson Ave., Suite 140
Somerset, NJ 08873-4120
(908) 560-9560/560-8850(Fax)

140 West 51st Street
New York, NY 10020-1203
(212) 484-4000/307-4387(Fax)

230 S. Broad St., Floor 6
Philadelphia, PA 19102-4106
(215) 732-5260/732-5002(Fax)

Four Gateway Center
Room 419
Pittsburgh, PA 15222-1207
(412) 261-3617/261-6055 (Fax)

115 Cedar Street
Providence, RI 02903
(401) 453-3250/453-6194(Fax)

205 South Salina Street
Syracuse, NY 13202-1376
(315) 472-5483/472-0966(Fax)

1150 Connecticut Ave. NW, 6th Floor
Washington, DC 20036-4104
(202) 296-8510/872-9574(Fax)

34 South Broadway
White Plains, NY 10601-4485
(914) 946-1119/946-2661(Fax)

Appendix 1

Midwest

205 West Wacker Dr., Suite 1000
Chicago, IL 60606-1212
(312) 346-2282/346-0135 (Fax)

441 Vine Street, Suite 3308
Cincinnati, OH 45202-2809
(513) 241-8434/241-8437 (Fax)

17900 Jefferson Rd., Suite 101
Middleburg Heights
Cleveland, OH 44130-3490
(216) 891-4741/891-4740(Fax)

1101 Walnut Street, Suite 903
Kansas City, MO 64106-2110
(816) 221-6401/471-5264 (Fax)

Ten Oak Hollow St., Suite 170
Southfield, Michigan 48034-7405
(313) 352-5500/352-3147(Fax)

514 Nicollet Mall, Suite 670
Minneapolis, MN 55402-1092
(612) 332-6545/342-2334 (Fax)

One Mercantile Center
Suite 2512
St. Louis, MO 63101-1614
(314) 621-7175/621-3730(Fax)

South

1360 Peachtree St., NE, Suite 270
Atlanta, GA 30309-3214
(404) 872-3022/881-1134(Fax)

428 East Fourth St., Suite 300
Charlotte, NC 28202-2431
(704) 347-0200/347-2804 (Fax)

Two Galleria Tower, Suite 1440
Dallas, TX 75240-6620
(214) 702-8222/490-9008 (Fax)

1001 Fannin St., Suite 1317
Houston, TX 77002-6707
(713) 739-1302/739-1702(Fax)

99 SE Fifth St., Suite 200
Miami, FL 33131-2501
(305) 358-7777/358-4931 (Fax)

221 Fourth Avenue North
Nashville, TN 37219-2111
(615) 256-5857/244-8570 (Fax)

650 Poydras St., Suite 1535
New Orleans, LA 70130-6101
(504) 522-8781/561-8041 (Fax)

201 East Pine St., Suite 800
Orlando, FL 32801-2742
(407) 648-1185/649-8668(Fax)

Appendix 1

West

1660 Lincoln Street
Suite 2150
Denver, CO 80264-2101
(303) 831-0823/832-3626(Fax)

810 Richards Street
Suite 641
Honolulu, HI 96813-4714
(808) 531-0541/533-2306(Fax)
In Guam:
(671) 477-1845/477-3178(Fax)

443 Shatto Place
Los Angeles, CA 90020-0994
(213) 383-6516/386-2251(Fax)

2601 Main Street
Suite 240
Irvine, CA 92714-6220
(714) 474-5090/474-5087(Fax)

333 E. Osborn Road
Suite 310
Phoenix, AZ 85012-2365
(602) 234-0950/230-2151 (Fax)

645 South 200 East
Suite 203
Salt Lake City, UT 84111-3834
(801) 531-9748/531-0660(Fax)

525 C Street
Suite 400
San Diego, CA 92101-5278
(619) 239-3051/239-3807(Fax)

417 Montgomery Street
San Francisco, CA 94104-1113
(415) 981-3901/781-8426(Fax)

1325 Fourth Avenue
Suite 1414
Seattle, WA 98101-2511
(206) 622-6435/343-5679(Fax)

APPENDIX 2

Checklist for initiating AAA arbitration.

(Reprinted with the permission of the American Arbitration Association.)

	By Demand For Arbitration	By Submission to Arbitration
Disposition of the Original Demand or Submission	Mailed to the respondent	Filed with the AAA in Duplicate
Copies Needed by the AAA	Three	Two
Copies Retained by the Parties	The demanding party retains one.	Each party retains one.
Signatures Required	An authorized person for the demanding party signs and lists his or her title.	Authorized persons for both parties sign, listing their titles.
Identification of Parties	The responding party should be clearly identified by official name and address.	Official names and addresses of both parties should appear, with signatures and titles.
Contract Clauses	Arbitration clauses should be quoted in full (may be attached separately if more convenient). Include date of the document.	Not applicable
The Filing Fee	$300 must be advanced by the demanding party. The balance is due in sixty days. The arbitrator later apportions fees.	The fee may be shared equally. The arbitrator later apportions fees.
Statement of Dispute	It should be brief but clear and include the amount claimed, if any, and the relief sought.	Claims and answers should be brief but clear and include the amount claimed, if any, and the relief sought.

154

Appendix 2

	By Demand For Arbitration	By Submission to Arbitration
Answering Statement	The respondent may mail the answering statement to the claimant and file two copies with the AAA.	See above.
Composition of the Arbitration Panel	The AAA will determine the number of arbitrators unless composition is stated in the arbitration clause.	The number of arbitrators desired may be stated. If not stated, the AAA will determine the composition of the panel.
Locale of Arbitration	If not provided for in arbitration clause, the demanding party should indicate its preference.	Locale should be indicated, if possible.

APPENDIX 3

The American Arbitration Association distributes numerous information booklets free of charge. These include the very useful 19-page *Commercial Arbitration Guide for Business People*; the 13-page *Guide to Mediation for Business People*; the more detailed 200-plus page *Business Arbitration - What You Need To Know;* and the 128-page *Business Mediation -- What You Need to Know*, both by Robert Coulson. The American Arbitration Association also publishes a free 31-page booklet entitled: *Drafting Dispute Resolution Clauses: A Pretrial Guide*.

INDEX

157

ABOUT THE AUTHOR

John Landrum is a partner at the New Orleans law firm of Milling, Benson, Woodward, Hillyer, Pierson & Miller. A graduate of Westminster College and the Georgetown University Law Center, Landrum is a member of the District of Columbia and Louisiana bars. He specializes in business litigation.

* * * * *

NOTE

It is not the purpose of this book to offer legal advice. The author's intent is to provide thought-provoking ideas based on generalized situations. One of these thoughts is that, in many instances, early legal advice is critical. This book is not a substitute for that specific advice.